SAVED!
A GUIDE TO SUCCESS
WITH YOUR SHELTER DOG

M. L. Papurt, DVM

With 80 photographs

Illustrations by Michele Earle-Bridges

BARRON'S

About the Author

M.L. Papurt, DVM, is a graduate of The Ohio State University School of Veterinary Medicine and has specialized in dog care since 1962. She has written many articles concerning animal health issues. Dr. Papurt has personally adopted over 20 dogs from shelters and has found homes for countless other dogs.

Photo Credits

Norvia Behling: front cover, inside front cover, inside back cover, pages 1, 19, 40 bottom, 47, 65, 69, 84, 96; Pilot Dogs, Inc.: page 3; Bob Schwartz: pages 4, 5, 10, 14 bottom, 15 top, 15 bottom, 32 top, 32 bottom, 49 top, 66, 78, 88, 105, 107, 119, 137, 139, 145, 146, 147; Jean Wentworth: pages 14 top, 29, 67, 78 bottom, 121, 156, 157; Betty Nenadal: page 42; Paulette Braun: pages 44, 75, 77, 78 top, 79, 112 top, 112 bottom; Toni Tucker: back cover, pages 46 top, 49 bottom; Barb and Randy Barick: page 123; Courtesy of Staff of Geauga Humane Society: pages 2 top, 6, 8, 11 bottom, 18 top, 18 bottom, 28, 37, 40 top, 41, 46 bottom, 80, all other photos by M.L. Papurt.

Dedication

For every person who went to a shelter, selected an abandoned dog, and helped it to become a member of society. And for you—each of you, who give a place in your heart to a homeless animal. Because you care, one more life is *saved.*

All inquiries should be addressed to:
Barron's Educational Series, Inc.
250 Wireless Boulevard
Hauppauge, New York 11788

International Standard Book No. 0-7641-0062-9

Library of Congress Catalog Card No. 97-7744

Library of Congress Cataloging-in-Publication Data
Papurt, Myrna L.
    Saved! : a guide to success with your shelter dog / Myrna L. Papurt.
        p.   cm.
    Includes bibliographical references and index.
    ISBN 0-7641-0062-9
    1. Dogs. 2. Animal shelters. 3. Dog adoption.
    I. Title.
    SF427.P215   1997
    636.7′081—dc21   97-7744
                                                  CIP

Printed in Hong Kong

987654321

Contents

Chapter One
Why Buy a Dog From a Shelter?

Introduction

Millions of dogs are homeless. Every classified section in any major newspaper contains a long column of pets for sale. The bulletin board of every veterinary hospital has notices of dogs and litters of puppies "free to a good home," and nearly everyone knows someone who would like to get rid of a dog that came to their yard and wouldn't go away. These are all good sources for a dog—if that particular dog just happens to fit into your lifestyle.

Buying a dog can be the best thing you have ever done. Your new dog can be a wonderful companion. It can be your buddy on walks and romps in the park. It can be company when you're alone and sad. It can warn you when someone approaches your house. It can ride with you in the car on a dark night. It can play with your children for hours on end. It can even keep you warm on a three-dog night.

Buying the *wrong* dog can be a disaster. It can tear up your house.

It can make a mess all over. It can bite the kids. It can bark incessantly. It can make you wish you never decided to get a dog.

There are literally thousands of dogs to choose from at animal shelters. Every year in the United States, *ten million* dogs pass through shelters, so the selection is practically unlimited. Your perfect dog is among these millions—all you have to do is find it.

Every county, every city, every village throughout the country has a

These dogs are waiting for new homes.

A playful collie-type is good with older children.

Beagles are common in shelters. They tend to roam unless properly confined.

dog-control system of some sort. Unless you live in a very isolated area, there are at least three or four animal shelters or humane organizations within less than 50 miles from your home. Each of these shelters will have dozens of dogs to

offer, and the population changes almost daily. There are puppies of every age, young adult dogs and older dogs, many of them purebred. There are big dogs and small dogs, dogs that are already housebroken; and some that are trained to stay off the couch and to come when called. Whatever type of dog you want; you can find at a shelter. This book is designed to help you select the right shelter dog and to make it truly your best friend.

The initial price of a dog might not be a major consideration to you, but these days it seems that everything costs twice what it should. Even if the price isn't a deciding factor, it's nice to get value for your money, isn't it? At an animal shelter, you really get that value.

The prices advertised in the classified section of the newspaper under "Pets for Sale" might surprise you. Good purebred dogs often sell for hundreds of dollars. Puppies cost the most and the most money must still be spent on them. Shelter charges, however, are very reasonable and often include important and expensive items. Your dog may have already received many of its necessary vaccinations. You may be given a certificate for free or discounted spay or neuter surgery. In some cases, the surgery may already be done, so you save time and trouble as well as money. A county dog license is nearly always included in the price of a shelter dog, eliminating that additional cost. Nowhere can you get more dog for less money.

When Not to Buy a Shelter Dog

Who shouldn't buy a shelter dog? The person who won't be satisfied with anything less than a winning show dog should stay away from shelters, as should the person who wants a field-trial competitor, although shelter dogs can be entered in obedience trials under some circumstances and many shelter dogs have become fine hunters. A person who must have a young puppy of a certain breed probably won't find it at a shelter. That person will have to part with a lot of hard cash to buy one from a breeder, but for someone who wants a good buddy, a shelter dog is the best choice.

A Dog Is Waiting

It is not the intention of this book to stress the terrible fact that there are too many dogs in the world, but you should be aware that more than ten million dogs enter shelters every year and fewer than five million of these dogs get out alive.

Many of those that don't get out are wonderful animals that deserve a chance to live. With luck, you'll

Arnie was rescued from a shelter and sent to Pilot Dogs in Columbus, Ohio, for training. He served as Shirley's eyes for ten years.

have your dog for many years, and every day of all those years you'll know you helped make a difference. That great companion by your side would be dead if you hadn't bought it at an animal shelter. This is a satisfaction you can't get anywhere else. If you want a dog, do yourself a favor: get a shelter dog. Choose from thousands—you'll get a big bargain and you'll save a life.

Chapter Two

Many Kinds of Shelters

Organizations dedicated to animal welfare have existed for more than a century, however, long before there were humane societies, there were dog pounds. According to a dictionary, a pound is an enclosure for the confinement of strays. In the early part of the century dog pounds were nothing more than a pen or enclosure in which stray dogs were kept. Most of these strays were captured by the sheriff when farmers reported dogs molesting their livestock, and since their owners had to pay a fine to reclaim the dogs, many of the impounded dogs were destroyed.

A typical suburban animal shelter.

The original purpose of dog license fees was to compensate owners of livestock that were killed by dogs.

The History of Animal Shelters

As long as most people lived on farms, dog pounds were adequate in dealing with stray and homeless dogs. When the country became primarily urban, however, stray dogs were no longer a problem only to livestock owners; they became health and safety problems to city dwellers, as packs of dogs damaged property, spread disease, and threatened children.

Before the nineteenth century, all animals were legally considered to be property and there were no laws that regulated their treatment. Animals were entirely at the mercy of their owners or harborers. The modern concept of a humane society dedicated to the prevention of animal abuse originated in Great Britain with the founding in 1840 of the Royal Society for the Prevention of Cruelty to Animals. The first humane society in the United States was the work of a single man, Henry Bergh. On February 8, 1866, Bergh proposed to the New York State legislature that a society be formed for the protection of animals and on April 10 of that year, the legislature passed the law to incorporate The American Society for the Prevention of Cruelty to Animals. On April 19 the state legislature passed an additional anti-cruelty law and the new ASPCA was given the power to enforce it. Henry Bergh and two assistants set out to alleviate the suffering and neglect of animals in New York City and, by doing so, started an anti-cruelty movement that has been joined by millions of people in this country in the last 130 years.

There are incorporated in the United States several huge humane societies and hundreds of smaller ones that are dedicated to the prevention of cruelty, neglect, and abuse of animals. Most of these organizations also operate shelters, although the primary function of the largest of them is to promote education and legislation to further humane goals. The American Humane Association in Englewood, Colorado, the American Society for the Prevention of Cruelty to Animals in New York City, and the Humane Society of the United States based in Washington, D.C., are among the leaders of the national humane groups. These organizations publish many written guidelines for the establishment and operation of animal shelters. They offer programs under which shelters are encouraged

This Labrador hopes to leave the shelter soon.

to meet a strict standard of excellence in animal care and control.

In spite of the availability of information and the influence of these national groups, there are no uniform regulations in the United States governing the operation of animal shelters. Each shelter is free to adopt or reject any and all suggestions and to form its own rules.

Two Types of Shelters

Government Shelters

Government-operated animal shelters are usually a function of a city or county. Government shelters are often called *city kennels* or *county kennels* and are run by elected or appointed dog wardens. Wherever the words "animal control"

Many shelters conduct training classes to help owners with their new dogs.

- They depend entirely on contributions to establish and run their shelters.
- Shelters operated by private humane societies can choose the animals they take into their shelters and can choose the people to whom they sell these animals.
- Dogs from private humane societies often have been vaccinated against contagious diseases and surgically sterilized.
- Many private societies require a signed contract with the buyer ensuring that any animal not spayed or neutered will have the surgery performed.

Private groups often use in their official titles the words, "humane society" or "animal welfare." Some private humane societies also operate with a contract with local government agencies to handle those animals that come under the control of the animal warden. Such societies are obliged to accept all animals sent to them by the warden, and are paid by the municipality, either per animal or per year. These societies may segregate the warden's animals from their own or may handle all animals as a single population. In effect, they function as a combination of private humane society and animal control agency.

Dogs from a humane society are likely to receive a fair amount of care and are less likely to be euthanized than dogs from an animal control agency. When you buy a dog from a private humane society, you often

appear, that shelter is government-funded and government-operated.

Government-run kennels have the following functions: they accept unwanted animals, pick up strays and injured animals, and quarantine dogs that bite. They keep stray dogs for a few days to allow owners to reclaim them, offer for sale those dogs that are not claimed, and euthanize those that are not sold.

City and county kennels are obliged to accept any and all unwanted or stray dogs, and ordinarily they must sell them to anyone who wants to buy a dog, although some states regulate the sale of animals to medical laboratories. Ordinarily, government kennels do not neuter or vaccinate the animals they sell, although there are some exceptions.

Private Shelters

Private humane organizations operate under a completely different philosophy and under completely different financial conditions:
- They receive no money from government agencies.

get free or discount spay or neuter surgery, free or low-cost vaccinations, a dog license, sometimes a collar and tag. When you buy a dog from an animal control officer, usually all you get is the dog. You have to bring your own leash and pay for your own spay. This is not to discourage you from going to the municipal kennels. Government-funded animal control agencies kill a much greater percent of their dogs than do humane societies. Humane societies try to rehabilitate and place as many dogs as they can; animal control officers are hired mainly to eliminate the unwanted. You should be aware of what you'll get and where you'll get it. Your best chance to find a nice, healthy, neutered, vaccinated dog is from a humane society. Your most compassionate choice is to search at the animal warden's—most of those dogs are going to die.

The Size of the Shelter

Just as the types of shelters differ, their facilities are of many kinds. Some are huge establishments with landscaped grounds and a large staff of professionals. Some demand an interview and information about your lifestyle before they will sell you a pet. Some want to be sure you won't neglect the dog, your landlord won't throw you out, and your spouse won't leave if you bring another dog home.

Other humane societies operate on a much smaller scale and a much more limited budget, but their staff is no less passionate about having each of their dogs be put in a loving home. Some "groups" consist only of a compassionate person who has two or three homeless dogs in the basement. Some consist merely of a telephone number to call if you want to contact a person with a dog to place. Each member of these groups is interested in only one thing: Saving as many lives as possible.

Exploring Your Options

How can you locate all the organizations in your area that place homeless dogs? Start with your local telephone book. Look under these headings:
• Animal Protection Organizations
• Animal Shelters
• Animal Welfare Organizations
• Dogs
• Humane Societies
• Kennels
• Veterinarians.

Veterinarians are not humane agencies, although a surprising number of them in rural areas are under contract with local governments to act in the capacity of animal control officers. Veterinarians often are very good sources for dogs needing homes for these reasons:
• Stray or unowned, injured dogs are often taken to the nearest veterinary hospital or clinic, and some veterinarians treat these dogs and place them if their owners can't be found.

- Many veterinary hospitals have a list of clients who would like to place dogs in new homes. Some hospitals have a bulletin board full of descriptions and telephone numbers. The veterinarians' secretary can also be a wealth of information.
- Veterinarians and their staff are often well acquainted with smaller dog-rescue groups that may not be listed in the local telephone book. These people might be able to put you in touch with many suitable dogs.

If you need more contacts, you can write to the American Humane Association (see page 157 for the address) for the section of the Directory of Animal Care Agencies that lists the shelters in your state. Bear in mind, however, that this list contains the addresses of almost 5,000 shelters nationwide, and although this list is continuously updated, it is by no means complete. Most of the information in the list is also in the local telephone book; since there is a charge for the AHA list, start with the phone book.

Annie is a shelter mascot. The personnel couldn't give her up!

Project BREED is a group of purebred dog fanciers that publishes a national directory of breed rescue groups. This organization offers only purebred dogs, and almost all of the dogs they offer for adoption will be adults. All will be spayed or neutered, sometimes at the recipient's expense. If you've always wanted a dog of a certain breed, or if you just want to see if one of your favorite breed is available, ask your library to get you the book, *Operation Pet Rescue,* look up your breed, and call its rescue group. You could find just what you want.

Don't neglect the classified advertisements in your local newspapers and in those of surrounding communities. Look under "Dogs" or "Pets for Sale." People who are forced to give up their pets but really care about them often run ads, such as "needs good home." Many people have found wonderful dogs through the classifieds.

Take your time. You're going to have your new dog for many years, so a few days of exploring all the sources is well spent. Ask each shelter, each humane society, and each county animal control officer what they offer. Are the dogs vaccinated? Are they neutered, or is the surgery subsidized? What is the cost of each dog, and does that include a county license? After receiving the answers to these questions, make up your mind where you want to look, pick a good day, and go look for your dog.

Chapter Three

Where Do All These Dogs Come From?

The American Humane Association, a national organization based in Colorado, publishes a yearly *Animal Shelter Reporting Study,* which details the activities of 3,000 shelters from all over the country. Since their figures are only estimated, the Association gives them as a range: in 1990 between 9 and 15 *million* dogs passed through shelters in the United States. Other sources are more optimistic, stating that "only" about 8 million is the more correct number. These are almost unbelievable statistics. Where do all these homeless dogs come from?

Shelters receive their dogs in one of the following ways: A very small percent of shelter dogs are seized by humane officers from abusive or neglectful owners. Almost all of the dogs at shelters are either brought in by their owners or they are picked up as strays. The American Humane Association estimates that about 40 percent of the animals are relinquished and 60 percent are picked up. This means that more than three million dogs every year are abandoned at shelters by their owners.

Of these three million, many are puppies resulting from accidental matings of pet female dogs that were not spayed and were allowed to run loose. The owners don't want all these puppies, and after each dog has given birth to several litters, the owners have no more friends or relatives to give them to. They just put them in a box and take them to the "pound." It's easy: They get rid of the pups, and the millions of little

This nice, young shepherd-type was found wandering on the highway.

lives become someone else's problem. "They'll find them a good home" is the rationalization of these people but they don't face the fact that often the pups are euthanized and their "home" is in a landfill or an incinerator.

Why Dogs Lose Their Homes

The rest of the millions of relinquished dogs come from a great variety of sources: Some owners die, some become ill, and some move and can't take their dog. But the majority are turned in simply because their owners didn't want them anymore.

Why would a person get a dog, keep it for months or years, and decide to get rid of it? The usual reason is that the owners are no longer willing to care for the dog or no longer willing to put up with its actions.

Too many puppies are abandoned at shelters.

Of the millions of dogs that are picked up as strays, nearly all of them are unwanted by their owners. Not many of them are truly lost and can't find their way home; owners who want to keep their dogs don't let them run loose and get lost. If their dogs accidentally get away, owners who value their dogs search for them and reclaim them from shelters.

Unfortunately, many people abandon unwanted dogs far from home. It's easier than driving to a shelter and they don't have to explain why they don't want the dog anymore. Untrained dogs, sick old dogs, litters of puppies, pregnant dogs—if they become a bother or an expense, some people will leave them to die without a thought to their fate.

Will You Buy a Problem Dog?

Does this mean that at least *some* of the dogs at every shelter were abandoned because the owners judged their behavior to be unacceptable? Yes, it certainly does. Does this mean that you have a good chance of buying a dog from a shelter that has unacceptable behavior? Certainly not!

Well, why not? There are two big reasons. First, sensible people are too smart for that, and wouldn't get a dog on impulse alone. Sensible people decide ahead of time what kind of a dog they want, and they don't buy a dog until they find the right one. Since they have literally hundreds of animals to choose from, it's easy for them to find one that will be a wonderful pet for them.

The second reason you won't get a dog with behavior unacceptable to you is that you can teach almost *any* dog you buy to behave correctly in your home, and while you are training it, you can prevent it from making mistakes.

Most Dogs Can Become Wonderful Pets

The people who abandoned the dog of your choice threw away the opportunity to own an obedient, responsive, affectionate companion. Either they didn't know how to handle the dog, or they refused to take the time and trouble to do it. Their loss is your gain.

If you buy a puppy, its only problem is that it was born unwanted. A puppy is like a human infant—it's a blank slate, and you only have to train it, not re-train it. The puppy has inherited certain behavior traits, but it has not had many bad experiences because it hasn't been alive long enough. The worst fault a shelter puppy can have is shyness or fear, which is the result of lack of human contact. With a puppy under eight weeks of age, you can easily overcome this problem in a few days by simply handling it gently when you feed it and by feeding it often.

If you choose an adolescent or adult shelter dog, you have to be

ready to change some of its behavior. The most common reason given for abandoning a dog is that it's "too much trouble." This really means several things: It is too "wild," it barks, it chews, it messes, it bites. All of these problems result from lack of correct handling by the former

Samson's owner couldn't keep him, but this ten-year-old Airedale-type still has lots of love to give to a new family.

This young collie-mix was adopted to be a pal for a ten-year-old child.

owner, and only one of these means anything at all to you, the new owner.

Avoid the Biter

Very few shelters offer for sale any dog that is an obvious biter, but shelters may not know if a dog will bite under circumstances that bring out its fear or aggressive traits. See Chapter 9 for information that will help you recognize which shelter dogs might bite.

The "wild" dog, the barker, the chewer, the dog that is not house-broken—are usually dogs from six months to two years of age. Their former owners obtained them as small puppies and did nothing to help them grow up to be good pets.

When the pups got to be "too much trouble," out they went. The owners will tell the children they'll get them another little puppy that will "be better behaved," but soon that puppy will be out as well.

These dogs that had problems in their former homes were just acting like normal young dogs. You probably won't ever know what your new dog's problems were, because you're not going to let any problems exist. The dog you choose from a shelter won't mess in your house or chew up your furniture. It won't bark all night or bite your kids. You're going to prevent unwanted behaviors and teach wanted ones. It's easy. All it takes is a little effort and common sense.

Chapter Four

Euthanasia—Yes, You *Do* Have to Read this Chapter

Euthanasia is a sugar-coated word for killing. The word comes from the Greek, and it means a "good death." But no matter how you look at it, there is seldom anything good about death.

Too Many Dogs

Too many dogs are killed by animal control agencies in the United States every year. Why is this necessary? How did this terrible situation come about?

The answer to both of these questions is very simple. Dogs can reproduce too fast. They have been allowed to reproduce to the point that there are not and never can be enough homes for all the dogs that are born.

Many of humans' compassionate actions have actually resulted in an increase in homeless dogs. Shelters find homes for thousands of puppies that otherwise would die of starvation and neglect. Many of the dogs that are saved grow up to become parents of still more unwanted puppies. In addition, scientists have developed vaccines to prevent most of the major bacterial and viral killers of dogs, allowing more to survive and reproduce. Today, food formulated especially for dogs is nutritious, available, and relatively cheap. Drugs eliminate the scourge of parasitism. Dogs live longer and thus are able to produce more puppies.

Feral Dogs

What would happen if none of these unwanted dogs were killed? Unwanted dogs have more litters than wanted ones because nobody cares enough about these dogs to confine them or to have them surgically sterilized. Imagine a sudden halt to the killing of dogs by animal control agencies. It's not a pretty picture. Within days, every shelter would be filled to capacity. There would be no place for people to take the dogs they didn't want to keep, and millions

The nice dogs shown here (and opposite page) may have been purchased from animal shelters.

of dogs would simply be abandoned to run loose and breed. These dogs would become *feral,* a term that describes a domestic animal gone wild. Packs of dogs would roam cities and rural areas, and other animals and children would be attacked by wild dogs scavenging for food. Dog excrement would litter the streets. Dog damage would be evident everywhere, and the bodies of dogs killed by cars would lie on the sides of the roads.

Eventually, the number of feral dogs would diminish as starvation and disease reduced the population to one which the environment could support. Is that what we want for our dogs?

Obviously not. Killing the excess dogs is, for now, the only answer.

Euthanasia Policies

Government Animal Control Shelters

Imagine yourself in the place of an animal control officer. Your job now is to impound dogs that nobody wants: strays, puppies, and those turned in by owners for various reasons. You must see that these dogs are housed for a few days, then you must kill those for which society has no room. Often, you or your employees must kill hundreds of dogs a week.

Some of these dogs are biters, unmanageable, or otherwise unsuited to be placed in homes. Some of them are old and sick. But the majority of the dogs you must kill are friendly and healthy. You have to kill them all, even the frisky little puppies. You jab the needle into their veins as they lick your face. How long would you last at that job?

It's no wonder that sorrow and guilt decimate the ranks of animal control workers. Society demands that their work must be done, but none of us is willing to take their places. The people who stay on the job must be tough. They must develop the philosophy to sustain them that death by lethal injection is much kinder than death from starvation and abandonment.

"No-Kill" Shelters

Because of human emotions of pity and concern, and because of the concept that all life is valuable, "no-kill" humane societies have found their way into the world of animal shelters. The idea behind these societies is laudable: Every sick, injured, abused, and abandoned dog will be given whatever it needs to restore it to good health and to find it a loving home.

Everyone admires no-kill humane societies. Donors feel that their contributions save the lives of dogs that other shelters would kill. People who could not bring themselves to work with dogs that might soon be dead are anxious to volunteer at these no-kill shelters. Sounds wonderful, doesn't it? But, unfortunately, no-kill humane societies have a terrible problem.

These no-kill shelters must be extremely careful about which dogs they take in. If they take in dogs that bite, if they take in dogs that are impossible to handle, if they take in dogs that are senile, horribly injured, or incurably ill, the true no-kill humane society, by its own decision, still cannot kill them. The shelters must keep these dogs until they can be taught not to bite, can be trained to be under control, can be cured of their illnesses, or until they die of their injuries or natural causes.

Injured and sick dogs are not the big problem, as some of these will die and many of the rest can be cured. The much greater problem is the unruly or biting dog. A few of these dogs can be improved by

training, but it takes an expert dog trainer a great deal of time and effort to accomplish this. Even after a humane society spends enormous amounts of time and money on each unsocial dog, there is no guarantee that a new home can be found or that the dog will be a success in any home.

While time, money, and kennel space are being expended on a dog that, at best, would be a marginal pet and hard to place in a home, the no-kill shelters must refuse dozens of healthy and friendly dogs because they have no room for them. Most of these dogs are abandoned to die or are taken to conventional animal control shelters where they are killed. For this reason, each no-kill shelter must make a decision whether to accept only animals that are readily adoptable. They must refuse the sick, injured, abandoned, and abused dogs if these dogs show signs of being unfit to be placed in homes. If humane societies accept such dogs, instead of being places to find a nice pet, the no-kill shelters risk becoming nothing but warehouses for the unadoptable. If there is a no-kill shelter in your area, inquire whether it screens its dogs before it accepts them, and if it offers for sale only dogs that can become good pets.

"Selective-Kill" Shelters

What is the perfect solution, kill or no-kill? Obviously, and unfortunately, the perfect solution does not exist. Many humane societies without a no-kill policy keep their resident dogs for only a designated length of time, after which those not sold are euthanized just as are the dogs of the animal control officer. Probably the nearest to ideal are those humane societies that operate with a "selective-kill" or a "limited-kill" policy. These organizations accept the injured, the abandoned, the sick, and the abused. Their shelter personnel evaluates each and every dog that they take in. These societies spare no reasonable effort to rehabilitate every adoptable dog, no matter how long it takes, but they euthanize those that are not suitable for new homes. They do not keep and try to place dogs that have undesirable behavior. Most humane societies realize that they cannot save every dog that enters their shelter. Instead, they use their money, space and time to save as many adoptable dogs as they can.

What Can We Do?

There are things that we, as dog lovers, can do to reduce this terrible killing.

- We can prevent the birth of dogs that are born only to die.
- We can allow our own dogs to reproduce only if they are purebred and among the very best of their breed. We can encourage other dog owners to do the same.
- We can go to a shelter and buy a dog that has no home. Each of us can save a life.

Chapter Five
Dogs and Humans Share Many Diseases

The partnership of humans and dogs has existed long before recorded time. Dogs were the first animal to be domesticated; they have been companions and allies of humans for at least 12,000 years. The association between *Canis familiaris* and *Homo sapiens* has been mutually profitable over millennia. But humans and dogs share more than their lives—they also share some diseases. People can get sick from dogs, and dogs can get sick from people. Of course, humans and dogs can also get sick from fish, reptiles, birds, and especially from others of their own species.

A disease shared by humans and animals is called a *zoonosis,* pronounced zoo-no-sis. The plural of zoonosis is *zoonoses,* pronounced zoo-no-sees. Zoonoses can be caused by viruses, bacteria, parasites, and fungi. Most of the zoonoses of dogs and man are relatively mild, but some can be killers of both species.

Rabies

Everyone fears rabies, and with good reason. This is the most deadly zoonosis of dogs and man. It is well known that this viral disease is spread by the bite of an infected animal and that it kills nearly all its victims. However, rabies is the zoonosis that modern medicine can most easily prevent.

All warm-blooded animals can get rabies, but it is primarily a disease of bats and wild carnivores such as skunks, raccoons, foxes, and coyotes. Rabies spreads when affected wild animals are crowded away from their home areas into new territories and take the disease with them. It is spreading so quickly in the United States that before long, no part of the American continent will be free of this disease.

The rabies virus damages the nervous system of the affected animal, causing it to act in many abnormal ways. Some animals with rabies appear to be paralyzed or partly

Large dogs (like those shown on this and the opposite page), are common at shelters. New owners have many choices.

paralyzed; some rabid wild animals act tame or confused, and some rabid animals appear to be highly aggressive. Some have a combination of signs: They may seem to be almost asleep, yet be aroused to a frantic attack by the slightest noise or touch. If an animal acts unusual, *never, never* go near it!

The *incubation period* of a disease is the interval between the time when a healthy animal becomes infected by the disease organism and the time the animal actually begins to get sick. The incubation period of rabies can be many days or even weeks, depending on the virulence (strength) of the particular viral strain and the resistance of the infected animal. In some cases, the incubation period of rabies has been found to be as long as six months; however, it is believed that the infectious rabies virus appears in the animal's saliva for only a few days before the animal shows signs of the disease. This is the reason for the ten-day quarantine period for dogs that bite. If the biting animal shows no signs of illness within ten days, it is considered that the infective virus could not have been present in its saliva at the time of the bite.

Rabies is most often brought to humans by domestic animals that come in contact with wildlife. Dogs that are wounded by rabid wild animals can become infected by the rabies virus. Then, when they go home and bite people or other domestic animals, they spread the sickness. However, no person or pet need get this terrible disease because there are very effective ways to prevent it.
• Vaccines against rabies are very effective, safe, and inexpensive. All dogs should receive rabies vaccines at three months of age. These vaccines should be repeated

as often as recommended by the manufacturer to keep the dogs' immunity at high levels.

- Pet animals should never be allowed to run loose. Loose dogs and cats can come in contact with infected wildlife or domestic animals, can become infected themselves, and can bring rabies back to their families.
- Everyone must avoid contact with all wild mammals. A wild animal that acts tame may act that way because of disease. Injured or sick wild mammals may have rabies.
- Nobody should handle stray dogs or cats without taking appropriate precautions. Children should stay away from any animal they don't know. Even if the animal acts normal, it might be in the early stages of disease.

Rabies in Shelter Dogs

What about dogs at animal shelters? Can you buy a shelter dog and feel sure that it isn't in the early stages of rabies? This is a very important question; the answer depends on the incidence of rabies in your area and the policies of the shelter.

You can feel confident about buying any shelter dog if you choose one that was turned in by its owner and was accompanied by a certificate of vaccination against rabies.

If you live in an area where rabies has not yet become common, you can buy a shelter dog with confidence even if you have no proof that it had a rabies vaccine. However, your dog should be vacci-

nated against rabies when you get it or immediately thereafter.

In areas with a high incidence of rabies, shelters often are prohibited from selling any dog that was a stray and might have been exposed to the disease. If you live in such an area, you should buy only an owner-relinquished dog that has been vaccinated against rabies and has not been allowed to run loose, or a puppy right out of its litter. If rabies is common in your area, you don't need to avoid buying a shelter dog, but be very careful!

Internal Parasites

Roundworms

The National Center for Disease Control in Atlanta, Georgia estimates that approximately 10,000 children are infected every year with roundworms from dogs and cats. Although fatalities are very rare, these parasites can do a lot of damage to the human body. Annually, about 750 children lose part or all of their eyesight as the result of roundworm infections.

The culprits in most of the cases are the many species of *Toxocara,* the common roundworms of dogs and cats. The larvae of these worms form cysts in the lungs, liver, kidneys, and muscles of affected adult dogs. Almost all dogs have some roundworm larvae in their bodies, but adult dogs usually show no signs of infection and seldom pass roundworm eggs in their stools.

When a female dog becomes pregnant, the roundworm larvae in her tissues become active. They migrate through the placentas into her developing pups and also into her mammary glands where they infect the newborn pups as they nurse. These larvae then become mature worms in the puppies' intestinal tracts. By the time the puppies are four weeks of age, the worms start to produce thousands of microscopic eggs that are passed in the puppies' stools. During the mother dog's pregnancy and while she is nursing her puppies, roundworms also mature in her intestines and pro-

duce thousands of eggs. The mother dog as well as her puppies will pass worm eggs in their stools.

Human infection with *Toxocara* occurs when children or adults accidentally get the microscopic eggs of this parasite into their mouths. This usually happens in one of two ways:

1. Children playing in yards where there are dog stools put contaminated objects, including their hands, in their mouths.
2. Children or adults handle puppies that are passing huge numbers of parasite eggs, and get the eggs on their hands from the infected puppies. Unless people are careful to wash their hands, they may accidentally ingest the eggs.

When a human swallows eggs of the *Toxocara* parasite, the eggs travel to the small intestine where they hatch into larval roundworms. These larvae migrate throughout the human body and invade nearly every tissue and organ. Two distinct syndromes of *Toxocara* infection are commonly recognized by the medical profession: *Visceral larva migrans* causes fever, changes in the blood, and an enlarged liver; *occular larva migrans* causes damage to the eyes.

Roundworms are a problem in all puppies, not only in those from animal shelters. Nearly every puppy is born with a roundworm infection that can affect people, so the same precautions should be taken with a puppy from a shelter and a puppy from any other source. Roundworms are not hard to control, but it takes persistence to control them properly.

- People, especially parents, must be educated to be aware of the danger of dog roundworms to their children.
- Areas in which children play must be protected from contamination with dog and cat fecal material. Dogs must not defecate in yards where children play.
- Roundworms must be eliminated from puppies by proper veterinary treatment.

Protection Against Round-worm Infection: When you buy a shelter dog, what should you do to protect yourself and your family from the *Toxocara* parasite? If you buy an adult dog, you should take the dog to your own veterinarian immediately. Even if the dog had been treated by the shelter for internal parasites, you should request that the dog be given at least one dose of a *broad-spectrum anthelminic,* a drug that kills many kind of worms. Your new dog's stool should be examined under a microscope at regular intervals until you are sure that it doesn't have worms in its intestines, and examined again at least once a year. Follow your veterinarian's advice.

When you buy a puppy from a shelter, you must assume it has roundworms and possibly other kinds of worms as well, and you must assume that it will pass worm eggs in its stool. Many, but not all, humane societies recognize this and treat every puppy with an anthelminic before it is offered for adoption. When you buy a shelter puppy, ask if it has received any treatment against worms, and write down the dates and drugs used so you can take the information to your veterinarian.

Even if an examination of your puppy's stool under the microscope reveals no eggs, your puppy should be treated for worms at two-week or shorter intervals until it is at least three months old. Regular preventive deworming is the safest and most practical way to be sure that your puppy will not pass worm eggs to your family. Worm medicines are safe, cheap, and not toxic to dogs, but be sure to use only those medications approved by your veterinarian for treating each condition, since the wrong medicine can harm or even kill your puppy. At the very least, the wrong medicine may not get rid of the worms, but may give you a false sense of security if you think the job has been done. If your veterinarian doesn't recommend routine deworming of puppies, even in the absence of a positive stool sample, seek another opinion and suggest that your veterinarian read the current literature on the subject from the American Veterinary Medical Association.

When you buy a young shelter puppy, there are a few precautions you should take during the weeks that the puppy is being routinely dewormed.

1. The first thing you should do is give your new puppy a bath.

Wash away all the fecal contamination that could be on its hair from its own stools and those of its littermates.

2. If your new puppy messes in its pen, clean it up thoroughly and wash the puppy again. Until all the worms are eliminated from its intestines, the puppy's stool may contain eggs. If the puppy licks up any of the eggs, it will become infected again.

3. Be especially careful to wash your hands after you handle a puppy that you are not sure is entirely free of worms. Have your children wash their hands, too. Veterinarians and their assistants who routinely handle puppies with *Toxocara* are not affected by the parasite because they recognize the problem and practice good hygiene. You and your chil-

dren won't be affected if you use reasonable care.

4. If your neighbor's dog has a litter of puppies, don't take your children over to see them, and especially don't let your children handle them. Remember, mother dogs and puppies are the ones most likely to pass roundworm eggs. Conscientious dog breeders start to treat both the mother dog and the puppies by the time the puppies are only two weeks old, even before the worms start to produce eggs.

An important note: The human pinworm, *Enterobius vermicularis,* is not the same as *Toxocara,* the dog and cat roundworm. Dogs don't get human pinworms, nor can they transmit them to people. Children and adults can get pinworms only from contact with other people who are infected with pinworms.

Hookworms

Both humans and dogs can harbor hookworms in their small intestines. The dog hookworm and the human hookworm are not the same species, but dog hookworm larvae in the ground can cause skin disease in children who walk barefoot or play in contaminated dirt. This is another reason to keep your pets' exercise areas and your children's play areas separate. Many *vermifuges* (another word for worm medicine) for dogs eliminate hookworms, roundworms, and other parasites at the same time, and prevent several problems at once.

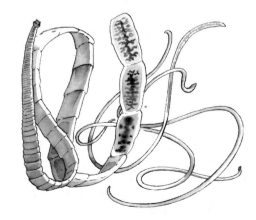

A tapeworm and roundworms.

Bacterial Infections

Bite Wounds

As many as 64 different species of bacteria have been found in the mouths of dogs. The mouths of humans also contain many kinds of bacteria, some of them the same species as those found in dogs. Bacterial infections are very seldom spread by dogs licking people or by sharing children's toys; it's bite wounds that cause the trouble.

When you buy a shelter dog, you get an animal that often has not had a perfect life. It may have been discarded by its previous owner for reasons that you probably will never know. It is of the greatest importance that you select a dog that is not likely to bite you or your family. Important information on how to do avoid buying a biter will appear in Chapter 9. *Never* deliberately buy a dog that bites.

Humans' jaws aren't very strong, but most dogs have very good biting equipment. Dogs have strong jaw muscles and big canine teeth that can cause puncture wounds and tissue damage. Puncture wounds can be very deep and hard to clean. Inadequate cleansing of wounds and insufficient removal of damaged tissue allow bacteria to grow and to produce severe infection. All but the most superficial bite wounds made by humans or animals should be seen and treated by a physician or veterinarian, depending on the species bitten.

Tetanus

Tetanus, or lockjaw is a disease caused by the bacterium *Clostridium tetani.* If untreated, it can kill all mammals, including dogs and man. The tetanus organism does not live in the mouth, but it is a common soil contaminant. The reason human bite victims are given a tetanus shot is that the organism can grow only in *anaerobic* conditions, in the absence of air. Bites, like other puncture wounds, often are deep enough so that air doesn't reach the bottom of the wound. This gives the tetanus bacteria a good place to grow. Humans and horses are relatively susceptible to tetanus; dogs and cats are relatively resistant to the disease.

Fecal Bacteria

Escherichia coli are the common fecal bacteria of both humans and dogs. Our bodies all contain this organism, and it usually does us no harm, but there have been cases of food-bourne human strains of *E. coli* causing several deaths. This is another important reason to prevent dog and human fecal contamination of your environment.

Skin Diseases

Ringworm

The ringworm organism, *Microsporum canis,* is a fungus that grows on the skin and hair of many animals. Cats are the species most likely to be affected. Humans who catch ringworm from animals are most often children who get it from kittens. Nevertheless, ringworm *does* occur in dogs, and can be transmitted to people.

The first sign of ringworm in dogs is usually scattered hairless patches on the head or legs. This is also the first sign of *demodectic mange,* a condition that never spreads to people. Your veterinarian can perform the easy tests necessary to differentiate these two skin conditions.

Dog ringworm is not a common problem. It is treated in both dogs and humans by applying medication to the skin and by giving tablets orally. While it may take weeks to eliminate all the ringworm organisms from an affected dog, modern veterinary science deals with this disease very well.

Sarcoptic Mange

Sarcoptic mange is a dog disease. *Scabies* is a human disease that is very similar to sarcoptic mange in dogs. Both are caused by a microscopic mite, both produce intense itching, and both are very transmissible from one animal or one person to another and from one species to another. Fortunately, both scabies on humans and sarcoptic mange on dogs are easy to cure. Medicated lotions are commonly used on humans, but the mites are best killed on dogs by a few doses of *ivermectin,* an oral or injectable drug.

Sarcoptic mange may be hard to diagnose on dogs by examining a skin scraping under the microscope because the mites that cause the disease are not numerous in the skin. Badly affected animals are covered with crusty sores, but some puppies with the disease might look normal but scratch themselves constantly. If your shelter puppy can't seem to stop scratching and your veterinarian can't find another reason, suggest that the pup be treated for sarcoptic mange, just in case that's the cause.

External Parasites

Fleas

Mark Twain made the remark that a few fleas were good for a dog because they kept it from worrying about being a dog, but that famous author was wrong—dogs with fleas are miserable and can scratch themselves raw. It's easy to tell if your dog is infested with fleas: Look for small dark creatures running through the hair on the stomach, the insides of the dog's hind legs, or on the back near the tail. Fleas run on dogs and cats, but jump a long distance from one animal to another.

Dog fleas live both on dogs and cats, but not on humans; however, they will bite people, usually on bare arms and legs. Their bites leave small itchy red spots. Fleas will bite men, but seem to prefer to bite women and children.

Fleas cause a great deal of skin disease in dogs and cats, and also carry the larval form of a tapeworm. When an itching dog swallows fleas as it chews its skin, it can be infected by this parasite. Human tapeworms are not the same. Humans can't get dog tapeworms even if they did swallow infected fleas. Bubonic plague, a flea-borne human disease, is carried by rat fleas, not the fleas of dogs and cats, even though fleas from rodents can get on dogs and from them onto people.

A tick and a flea.

Lice

Lice (singular: louse) are skin parasites that are very *host-specific.* This means that dog lice live only on dogs, human lice live only on humans. Dog lice may accidentally get on a person, but they cannot live there. The head lice your child may bring home from school came from a classmate, not from a dog.

Lice are very small, usually white or grayish-white. They are relatively stationary on their host, and don't run through the hair like fleas. Louse eggs are called *nits* and can be seen attached to individual hairs. Lice are readily transmitted to other animals of the same species by contact, so if you buy a puppy and find lice on it, treat all your dogs. Your veterinarian has shampoo that will kill lice; it's almost the same preparation that is used on children.

Ticks

Ticks are parasites of many kinds of animals, including dog and man. These creatures are not insects, but *arachnids,* related to spiders. Ticks pierce the skin of their host with their mouthparts and suck until their abdomens are full of blood. Blood-filled female ticks then drop off the host animal and lay their eggs in the ground. Newly-hatched ticks are called *nymphs;* they are very agile in jumping onto a host animal. After a few feedings on different animals, nymphs molt (shed their skins) and become adult ticks.

Many species of ticks cause disease or carry disease caused by other organisms to both man and dog. Rocky Mountain Spotted Fever, a rickettsial disease, is carried by the American dog tick, the American wood tick, and the Lone Star tick. This disease is most common in the southern states. Lyme disease, a bacterial infection, is carried by the deer tick. Tick paralysis is caused by toxins actually secreted by some ticks. The animal or person affected with tick paralysis gradually becomes more and more paralyzed and can die from respiratory failure. If the tick is removed in time, the victim soon recovers.

If you live in an area where ticks are common, you might find some of them on the dog you buy from a shelter. Usually, you can feel ticks if you check for tiny lumps on your dog's head, in its ears, and between its toes. The ticks feel and look like little tumors filled with blood. They vary in size depending on the species of the tick and the length of time the ticks have been feeding on the dog's blood. The males don't swell up with blood; they resemble little fat spiders with flat bodies and eight tiny legs. Once female ticks attach to skin, they don't move until they are full of blood; then they drop off into the environment. Remember, tiny dark creatures that run through fur or that jump are fleas, not ticks.

It is important to get rid of the ticks before they multiply in your house or yard, and ticks are very resistant to many chemicals. If you find ticks on your dog, scrape or pull them off immediately, but not with your bare hands. Protect yourself by wearing rubber gloves or grasping them through a couple of layers of plastic wrap. If you want to save the ticks to take to your veterinarian to be identified, drop them into a screw-top jar and screw the lid on tight. If you don't want to save them, smash them through the plastic wrap after you've picked them off the dog, then flush them down the toilet.

Old wives' tales tell you to hold a lighted match to a tick, or daub it with kerosene, to "make it let go."

Don't worry about this; just yank the ticks off your dog. You can treat the spots where the ticks were attached with rubbing alcohol or tincture of iodine if you're worried about infection. If any parts of the ticks remain in the dog's skin, the parts will soon dry up and fall off. Don't try to use eyebrow tweezers to remove ticks. It is difficult to pick a tick off a dog with tweezers without squashing the tick and releasing blood that might be infectious.

When they first get on a dog, ticks are very tiny and hard to find, but after a day or so of feeding on the dog's blood, they get much larger. Be sure to check your new dog for ticks at least once a day for three or four days, because you may have missed the smallest ticks the first time. You'll be able to find them later when they get full of blood and enlarge.

Summary

- Don't even consider buying a shelter dog that could be in the incubation stage of rabies.
- If you live in an area where rabies is prevalent in wildlife, talk to the shelter personnel and find out the source of any dogs you might consider buying.
- Buy only a dog that has had no chance to be bitten by a rabid animal.
- Have your shelter dog receive a rabies vaccine immediately after you buy it.

Puppies from all sources, not just shelters, present the danger of roundworm infection to your children. This is not a reason to avoid buying a puppy but it *is* a reason to take appropriate precautions until you are sure your puppy is no longer passing roundworm eggs. Have your veterinarian start a program of regular deworming, even if there are no worm eggs found in the puppy's stool. Keep the puppy and its environment very clean and have your children wash their hands every time they handle their pup.

Nothing in life is completely safe. Any dog you get from any source could have some problems. Be cautious when buying any dog but there is no reason to be more cautious when buying a shelter dog than when buying a dog somewhere else. So buy that dog, but use your head.

Chapter Six
The Question of Health

Buying a sick dog is a bad way to start a good relationship; you want your new dog or puppy to be in perfect health. Dog owners bond with their new pets the instant they choose them, and to find that they've bought a sick dog can be devastating. How can you be sure the dog you buy isn't suffering from some disease or injury that will need expensive, time-consuming treatment? Or worse, a condition that might be fatal? You can't be completely sure, but you can take some precautions.

A healthy dog is alert and active.

Canine Viral Disease

A big problem with buying a shelter dog is the probability that the dog you choose will have been exposed to one or more sick dogs, and if your new dog has no immunity, it might be in the incubation stages of a serious medical condition. Most of these important canine diseases are caused by viruses.

A number of viral diseases affect only dogs and dog-like animals, but do not affect people. Canine *distemper* and canine *parvovirus* are among the worst, and are often fatal. Other viral diseases of dogs are *coronavirus, viral hepatitis, parainfluenza, bordetella* and *canine bacterial leptospirosis.* These diseases are spread from dog to dog by contact with sick dogs or virus-bearing substances in the environment. Distemper spreads through air-born water droplets. Parvovirus spreads through microscopic particles of fecal material. Dogs that develop these diseases have no antibodies in their blood that destroy the viruses.

As with human disease, some dog diseases are more serious than others and some diseases are more easy to control than others. Distemper and parvovirus are cften fatal, even when heroic medical treatment is given. Coronavirus, parainfluenza, and bordetella are less often fatal, although the victims of these diseases can get very sick.

Immunity to Viral Disease

A dog can develop immunity to a specific disease in one of three ways:

1. A dog that has recovered from a viral disease develops in its body substances called *antibodies* against the specific virus. If the dog again comes into contact with the same virus, these antibodies will destroy the virus and prevent the dog from getting the disease again.
2. When a dog is vaccinated, it receives a substance that contains the disease organisms that have been altered in such a way that they cannot produce the actual disease. The weakened organisms contained in vaccines "fool" the body into making antibodies that protect the animal from the real disease. Modern vaccines are usually formulated to protect the dog from several diseases at once.

Just as with human diseases, some conditions impart a lasting immunity and some diseases do not. A dog that recovers from distemper probably is immune to that disease for life, but a dog that recovers from one of the several respiratory diseases (bordetella, parainfluenza, and other cough-causing viruses) may get sick again if it comes in contact with a contagious dog.

3. Puppies are born with no antibodies in their blood and no protection against disease. If the mother dog is immune to certain diseases, she will pass that immunity to her pups in the form of *maternal antibodies* that are contained in *colostrum,* a mother dog's first milk. Puppies can absorb these *maternal antibodies* only for the first six or eight hours of their lives; this is why it is so important that newborn puppies nurse promptly.

The temporary protection that pups get from their mother's milk is called *passive immunity* because the pups' bodies don't make it, they just receive it from the milk. When the antibodies from the mother's milk are gone, the pups are susceptible to developing the actual disease.

Adult dogs need only to receive a booster vaccine.

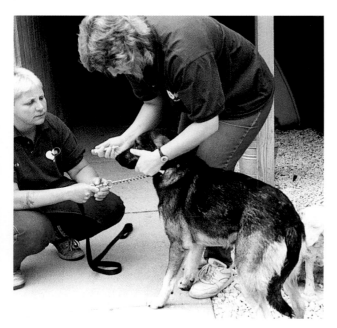

Shelter technicians are giving this young dog an intranasal vaccination against respiratory diseases before it sets foot inside the shelter.

Not all mother dogs pass on the same amount of passive immunity, so there is a variation in the length of time (usually five to twelve weeks) that puppies are protected from contagious disease by the antibodies in their mother's milk. Until the mother dog's antibodies are gone from the puppies' bodies, the puppies will not only be protected against the disease, but against the action of vaccines as well. The maternal antibodies will destroy the vaccine just as if it were the actual virulent disease organisms. For this reason, it is important that puppies be vaccinated after their maternal antibodies are gone, but before they come into contact with disease organisms. Puppies should be vaccinated repeatedly, usually at two-week intervals, until they are twelve

weeks old. This insures that they received a vaccine that was not destroyed by left-over maternal antibodies.

Viral Disease in Animal Shelters

Animal shelters are like public schools in that every child is exposed to every other child. If one child comes to school with a cold, the other children may catch it; if one child has measles, the other children are at risk of getting measles also. Every child entering public school is required to be vaccinated against the worst childhood diseases, but, unfortunately, there is no such requirement for dogs entering animal shelters.

Since the dogs at animal shelters are from many and varied sources, you should assume that the dog you choose from a shelter has been exposed to whatever viral and bacterial diseases are prevalent in your area. Does this mean that the dog you buy is going to get sick? Maybe.

Many owner-relinquished dogs at shelters have received at least some vaccinations. Strays may have, but there is no way of knowing their vaccination status. Almost all litters of puppies taken to shelters have had no medical treatment; if their owners cared enough about their dogs to have them vaccinated, they wouldn't have let them have unwanted puppies in the first place.

Many humane societies and some animal control shelters administer vaccines to their dogs, but some do not. Some shelters vaccinate only puppies; some vaccinate only dogs that appear to be the best candidates for adoption; some shelters vaccinate only dogs and puppies after they are adopted; some vaccinate no animals at all. Vaccines are expensive and must be administered by people with special training, and many shelters do not allot the money for vaccines, even for the dogs most at risk of disease.

Incubation Period of Disease

After a dog or pup with no immunity has been exposed to a contagious disease, it takes a few days for the organisms to multiply in its body and make the animal sick. This is called the *incubation period*. For most diseases, the incubation period is five to ten days. After a dog or pup has received a vaccine, it takes a few days for its body to make the antibodies to protect it from the real disease organisms. Ideally, a dog should be vaccinated at least a week before it is exposed to other dogs that could be sick. This is seldom possible at animal shelters.

If a dog or puppy is vaccinated when it enters the shelter, its body starts to make antibodies at the same time that it is potentially exposed to disease organisms from any sick dogs that might be there. In most, but not all cases, the dog's immunity from the vaccine will develop more quickly than the actual disease organisms and the dog will be protected.

Before you buy a shelter dog or puppy, you should find out about its vaccination status. No dog, ever, has had all its shots, because many vaccines are given in a series and most vaccines require periodic boosters. These are the questions you should ask about any dog you're considering:

1. What is the age of this dog or puppy? Almost all puppies under five weeks will have enough maternal antibodies to be protected from contagious diseases. Dogs over two years that appear healthy are often (but not always) immune to most of the diseases because they have been vaccinated in the past or they have had the disease and have recovered.

2. Did this dog or puppy have any vaccinations before it entered the shelter? The answer will usually be, "No," or "We don't know."

3. Did the shelter give this dog or puppy any vaccines? If so, were the vaccines against several diseases? If the puppy was vaccinated at the shelter, you will probably find that it received vaccines against all or most of the diseases common in your area.

4. When was the vaccine given? If the puppy was at the shelter for several days before it was vaccinated, it is more likely to be in the incubation stage of a disease than one that was vaccinated as soon as it entered the shelter.

5. If the puppy is under twelve weeks old and has been at the shelter more than two weeks,

Lucky dogs will be vaccinated before they are given up for adoption.

How should you evaluate this information? It's different if you're buying a puppy than if you're buying a mature dog.

- If you choose an owner-relinquished dog or puppy that has a record of vaccinations, you're usually in the clear. The shelter will give you a copy of the dog's record to take to your veterinarian. Make an appointment for your dog to get whatever boosters it needs.

- If you choose a dog over two years old that has no record of vaccinations and no vaccinations were given by the shelter, it is fairly safe to assume that the dog has some immunity to whichever diseases are common in your area, but take it to your veterinarian and get its vaccines immediately.

- If you choose a puppy under six weeks old that has had no vaccines, it probably has enough immunity from its mother to be protected, but it still should be vaccinated within two weeks.

- If you choose to buy a puppy older than six weeks or a young adult dog, and if you buy it from a shelter that does not vaccinate, you risk buying a sick dog. If you buy a young dog like this from a shelter that administers vaccines only to animals after they are sold, you risk buying a sick dog. A vaccine given several days after exposure won't protect the dog, because the disease organisms have had several days' head start

was the vaccine repeated? This is important because a very young pup may have received its initial vaccine when its body was unable to respond correctly. To be sure it is protected, young puppies should receive repeated vaccines until they are at least twelve weeks old.

to multiply before the vaccine can protect the dog.

Do a little research before you go looking for a new dog. Telephone the shelters in your area and ask if they vaccinate their dogs, and which dogs they vaccinate. Telephone your veterinarian or other veterinarians in the area and ask if their office has seen many sick dogs or puppies from local shelters. Ask for their recommendations about each shelter. In most cases, you won't have to talk to the doctor; the secretary will know. With this information you can limit your search to shelters where you will have confidence that the dog you choose will be healthy. Remember: no shelter, no matter how carefully it vaccinates, is infallible. Nobody, not even a veterinarian, can tell when a dog is in the incubation stages of some diseases. If you buy a dog or puppy from a shelter that has an adequate vaccination program, you minimize your risks of getting a sick one to not more than the risks you take with buying a dog from any other source. However, if you buy a young animal from a source that does not vaccinate, you might be in trouble.

Danger Signs of Disease

Signs of disease in a new dog may appear gradually, so even if the dog you buy has received vaccines, watch it carefully for at least a week. One day you might notice that your puppy seems to be not quite up to par, the next day it's a

First Signs of Disease

- Refusal to eat, or eating much less.
- Listlessness.
- Reluctance to play.
- Sleeping much more.
- Elevated body temperature.
- Vomiting.
- Diarrhea.
- Coughing.
- Gagging.
- Harsh breathing.
- Discharge from the eyes or nose.

bit more listless, and by the third day, the pup is definitely sick. Or the signs might appear acutely. Suddenly, the dog that seemed to be in fine health is vomiting and has diarrhea. Acute onset of disease usually indicates an emergency. Rush the dog to your veterinarian. If there is a delay of even an hour before treatment is started, the disease process may become irreversible and the dog may die.

Fever: One of the first signs of the onset of disease in a dog or puppy is an elevated body temperature, just as one of the first signs of a sick child is a fever. Humans' normal body temperature is usually considered to be 98.6°F or 37°C (the place marked with a little arrow on a regular human thermometer). A dog's body temperature is higher than that of a human, and there are more normal variations, depending on the size, age, and activity of the dog. Nevertheless, the normal temperature of a dog taken with a regular human rectal thermometer should be between 101° and 102°F (38.3° to 38.9°C). Anything over 102.5°F (39°C) is considered a fever and anything over 103°F (39.4°C) should alert the owner to something seriously wrong.

Respiratory Distress: Respiratory diseases among dogs in a shelter, like the common cold among children in school, are very hard to control because the diseases are caused by many different viruses and are spread very easily. Because these diseases are so common in shelters and kennels, they are often called "kennel cough," or lumped together and called the "kennel-cough complex." Your new dog or puppy might develop a slight cough but continue to eat and play; it needs only time to get over it, just as a child who comes home from school with a runny nose. Or your dog may cough severely, refuse to eat, and run a fever; it needs veterinary attention just as a sick child needs to be seen by a pediatrician. The key to differentiating between the two is to watch closely to see if the patient is getting worse or if it has any of the abnormal signs listed earlier. If it has, call the veterinarian.

Vomiting and Diarrhea: A dog that has a viral disease usually vomits only whitish or yellowish fluid stomach contents because the dog feels too sick to eat solid food, even though it may drink water. Diarrhea accompanies nearly all viral diseases at the onset. The sudden appearance of black, foul-smelling diarrhea is very serious. It often is the first sign of canine intestinal viral disease, and can progress rapidly to life-threatening dehydration.

Internal and External Parasites

The shelter that vaccinates all the dogs it offers for adoption is most often the shelter that administers appropriate worm medications to its dogs, and is most often the shelter that treats its dogs for external parasites such as ticks and fleas (see Chapter 5). Ordinarily, the presence of parasites is not a reason to reject any dog as these things can be eliminated without too much trouble. Nevertheless, ask at the shelter if the dog you choose has been checked or treated. Whether the answer is yes or no, take the dog into a strong light and look it over for fleas and ticks *before* you allow it anywhere in your house except in its own enclosure. If any external parasites are present, use appropriate dips, shampoos, sprays, or powders on your dog to get rid of the parasites before they multiply. These products are available from your veterinarian or from a pet supply store. If any parasites or their microscopic eggs drop off the dog in its own area, you will have only that one small place to treat.

It is very unlikely that you will buy a dog with serious skin disease, because affected dogs look obviously unhealthy. If your new dog scratches all the time and you can't find any reason for it, or if you find non-itchy bald spots on your dog, have your veterinarian check it. Almost all these conditions are treatable and curable.

Canine Heartworm

Canine heartworm is just what the name implies—worms that live and grow in the chambers of the heart and major blood vessels of dogs. Obviously, this is a terrible place for an animal to have worms because the parasites can cause serious circulatory problems and can lead to the death of the affected dog.

Heartworm is spread by mosquitoes. When a mosquito sucks the blood of an infected dog, it also sucks up some of the microscopic immature form of the heartworm, called *microfilaria*. The mosquito passes these microfilaria to the next dogs it bites, and eventually the microfilaria develop within the host dog's body into large worms in the heart and blood vessels. These worms then produce more microfilaria that circulate in the dog's blood and are sucked up by mosquitoes that bite the infected dog. This continues the cycle.

Dogs can have heartworm for a long time until their circulatory systems become so clogged with parasites that they show signs of the disease. Cough and exercise intolerance are the first signs of serious heartworm infection. Some shelters test all the dogs they offer for adoption for the condition. Some shelters treat those dogs found to be infected; some shelters simply euthanize them. Almost all dogs with heartworm can be treated successfully if the condition is discovered before the dog shows signs of illness, but if the condition goes untreated, eventually the dog will die. Although heartworm now can be treated on an outpatient basis, it's up to you whether you want to risk buying a dog that may need rather expensive medical treatment. Before you buy, ask the shelter about how it manages this problem.

Hip Dysplasia

Dys is the Greek prefix for bad, and *plasia* is form: hip dysplasia means badly formed hip joints. Hip dysplasia is an inherited condition commonly found in large-breed dogs, and it can cause a dog with the condition to become severely lame in its rear legs. Hip dysplasia can be completely unnoticeable, serious enough to cause the dog significant pain, or anything in between those extremes. The affected dog is normal at birth; if the condition is serious, the puppy might be lame by the time it is three months old.

Mixed-breed dogs can have hip dysplasia, but it is more common in purebreds because the condition depends on the action of several genes. Since purebred dogs are

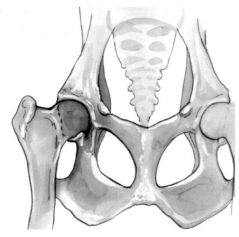

X-ray of a dog with normal hips. More than half the ball of the hip joint fits into the socket of the pelvis.

the dog is at least two years old. If you buy a dog over 18 months old and it walks and runs normally, chances are that it will never be troubled by malformed hip joints.

If you buy a young puppy of a large-breed type, your veterinarian may be able to make an educated guess about the condition of its hips by observing the gait of your puppy after it is five or six months of age. If there is any reason to think that your puppy might develop hip dysplasia, the veterinarian could make suggestions to help minimize the problem. One suggestion will be to control the weight of the growing pup to reduce strain on the weak joints. In mixed-breed dogs, hip dysplasia is seldom a serious condition.

more likely to have the same genetic makeup, purebred puppies are more likely to inherit the genes for hip dysplasia from both parents.

Hip dysplasia can only be diagnosed by X-ray; and the X-rays show the extent of the condition only after

Injuries

Humane societies and animal wardens receive many injured animals. Some shelters euthanize any dog that needs medical treatment; some treat only those with relatively minor injuries; some go to great trouble and expense to treat and rehabilitate all the injured dogs they accept. Depending on the policy of each shelter, it might offer for adoption dogs recovering from broken or amputated legs, dogs with an injured or missing eye, or dogs with other kinds of physical defects. Be aware that what is a handicap to a person may not be to a dog.

Amputees: A dog with three legs is not in any way self-conscious

This dog has hip dysplasia. Only a little of the ball is contained within the pelvic joint cup, and the ball is flattened and deformed.

about its appearance, nor will it be in any way impaired in running and leaping. Three-legged dogs, as soon as they recover from the surgery, act just like four-legged dogs; they can be guard dogs, hunting dogs, great pets, drug sniffers, whatever. Only racing greyhounds and sled-dogs would be in any way handicapped by the loss of a leg.

Dogs that had a leg amputated do not need a prosthetic limb, and in fact, should not have one. A dog will regard an artificial leg as an encumbrance, and will chew it off. Remember, a three-legged dog still has one more leg than you have. If you see a nice dog that has had an amputation, don't hesitate to buy it, if it's available. Amputees in the dog world usually are adopted quickly. Owners feel especially generous about giving these dogs a home.

Dogs with Only One Eye: A dog with adequate sight in one eye will function just as well as one with two good eyes but, as with a person with sight in only one eye, precautions must be taken to protect the remaining eye. This is only a consideration in cases where one eye has been affected by a congen-

ital condition such as in-turned eyelashes that rubbed on the cornea. In such cases, the dog's remaining eye should be evaluated by a veterinary ophthalmologist and appropriate intervention taken before damage is done. Dogs that lost an eye through trauma will function just fine with only the eye that remains, so don't be reluctant to choose that dog.

Notice the cast on this little dog's back leg. She made a complete recovery and got a wonderful new home.

Chapter Seven

Decide What You Really Want

Remember the old proverb: Act in haste, repent at leisure. Don't act in haste when you buy a dog. When you get a dog that fits your lifestyle, your environment, and your family, you'll have a wonderful relationship. When you get a dog that doesn't fit, you'll have aggravation and disappointment. At best, buying a dog is a gamble—let's see how to load the dice in your favor.

Picture the Perfect Dog

Nobody should try to tell someone else what kind of a dog to buy, what breed, type, age, or sex. All dogs are different and all owners are individuals. Each buyer should feel free to choose the dog he or she will most enjoy owning.

Picture the perfect dog for you. If you always liked Aunt Tillie's Fifi, make a list of all the ways you want your new dog to be like Fifi. If you like to toss Fifi's ball for her, write on your list, "very playful" as one of the things you want. If you like Fifi

because she's small, write, "not over 30 pounds (13.6 kg)"

If you like Fifi because she ignores the mailman, write "Never barks even if people approach the house." If you like Fifi because she sits on your lap, write "very affectionate." When you have described exactly what your perfect dog should be, you'll have at least eight or ten items on your list. You can have 20 or more if they're important to you and your family.

When you've completed your list, it might look something like this:

1. Shepherd-type, like the neighbors' "Queenie."
2. Adult weight 50 to 75 pounds (23 to 34 kg)
3. Female, black and tan, ears that stand up.
4. Barks at people approaching the house.
5. Any other traits that are important to you.

Your list may look nothing like that. You might want a completely different dog:

1. Not over 20 pounds (9 kg) in weight.

2. Short hair; requires little grooming.
3. Never growls at anyone, especially children.
4. Goes for walks around the neighborhood with Grandpa without pulling or tugging on the leash.

Or you might even want a dog like this one:

1. Male; long-haired.
2. Can live outdoors all year.
3. Will bark and growl at anyone who approaches the property.
4. Must look impressive and weigh at least 75 pounds (34 kg).

Once you have completed your list of characteristics, decide on which ones you're willing to compromise and how much you'll compromise. For example, if you'd like a dog smaller than 20 pounds (9 kg) and you find one that weighs 30 pounds (13.6 kg) but is otherwise suitable, will you compromise on the size? If you see a shepherd-type female, black and tan, but the ears flop, does that really matter to you?

Then decide on which traits you absolutely will not compromise. The most important one is likely to be "won't bite family members." Your personal list will have others.

Perfect dogs exist, but seldom at shelters. Except for unusual and often tragic situations such as the death of its owner, the perfect dog stays in its original home for life. But shelters are bursting with thousands of dogs that are almost perfect or will become perfect if given the chance. Dogs are discarded for

This cocker spaniel is just one of many purebreds that can be found at shelters.

the most unimportant reasons—reasons that a new owner can correct with little time or effort. With your list and an open mind, you will find your own potentially perfect dog waiting for you.

Size Is Important

You're going to live with this dog. Consider your space, time, and money when you choose it. If you have a tiny apartment, if you weigh 97 pounds (44 kg), if you work twelve hours a day, or if you're on a tight budget, you aren't likely to be successful with the same dog as a 180-pound (14 kg) man who works at home on his farm. Your lifestyles are different and your dog must fit

Want a watchdog? This Rottweiler looks fierce, but he's not.

These Jack Russell puppies will make fine pets.

your circumstances as well as your tastes.

The first consideration is the dog's size. Many people have a marked preference for a large dog but don't have a big house or yard. If you're one of them, compromise.

Get a medium-sized dog that resembles the large breeds you admire, or get a large dog with a quiet personality. You'll be dissatisfied if you always wanted a German shepherd and you buy a little terrier just because you read that terriers are good in small houses, but you might be delighted with a small shepherd-type dog that looks like your ideal but of a more manageable stature.

The Dog's Living Quarters

You will need an enclosure in which to keep your new dog until you get it trained to live with you. This area is called a Safe Space because, when the dog is in it, the dog is safe from harm and your property is safe from any damage the dog could do. You'll learn more about this in Chapter 11, but for now, you have to plan where this Safe Space will be, and the size of the dog dictates the size of the Space.

Of course, a puppy needs a smaller Space than the same dog will need as an adult, but even if you get a puppy, calculate on the basis of its full-grown size so that you don't have to make a larger Space later. A Safe Space need not, in fact, should not, be large enough for the dog to romp around in, but it must be big enough for it to lie down comfortably. A roomy wire cage will do for a small dog, but for a Great Dane, you probably need at least a 6 by 6 foot (1.83 m) pen.

Plan where you will locate your dog's Safe Space. It can be located wherever it is most convenient, but it's much better for the dog's social adjustment if the Space is where family members spend most of their time. If you can't spare the room in the kitchen or bedroom, (yes, the bedroom *is* a good place) and you're getting a really big dog, a dry and light garage or basement will do. Even a barn is satisfactory, if you have one and are planning for an outdoor dog.

Your Physical Capabilities

How big a dog can you physically handle? In most cases, this is not a major consideration because the average person can control the average dog. However, a dog can pull more than its own weight on a leash since dogs have four feet on the ground. If you're very unaverage physically, you might think this over before choosing a dog. For example, a 97-pound (44 kg.) person might have a problem training a 100-pound (45.4 kg) dog. Someone who has difficulty bending over or stooping might not want a toy-size dog that needs to be lifted into the car.

Space for Exercise

Remember, a big dog needs a big area for exercise. A half-hour of vigorous play in the house will be fine for a 10-pound (4.5 kg.) dog, but the same half-hour of play in the house with a 60-pound (27 kg.) dog might wreck the furniture. If you have a yard, your dog can play outside, even on a long leash. If you don't have a yard, get a sedentary dog, or plan to do a lot of walking.

This alert Belgian shepherd mix is ready for a new owner.

Consider Your Time and Your Budget

You will read books that tell you that, if nobody is home all day, you don't have time for a dog. You shouldn't get a dog or you should hire somebody to come in during the day and take care of it. Nonsense. It would be perfect if you didn't have to go to work, wouldn't it? It would be perfect if you had unlimited time, space, and money to spend on your pets, but life seldom is perfect for dogs or for people. However, just because life isn't perfect doesn't mean that you can't have dogs; you just have to arrange the situation to fit the circumstances. Think of it this way: The dog that you take from a shelter and give a good, if not perfect, home will be alive and enjoying itself. The dog that you don't take, might be dead.

If your time is limited, get an adult dog. A puppy that is left alone all day can't learn how you want it to act. It could take months before you reach the same comfortable relationship with a puppy that you would have with an older dog in a matter of days. Let someone with more free time raise the puppies.

Except for professional grooming and the amount of food it needs, the cost of owning one dog is very much the same as another. Each needs the same vaccinations and other veterinary services, although some one-time things, like spaying, might cost more for a very large dog. The cost of a dog license is the same for all dogs, regardless of size, but in some areas it may be different for males and females

Coat Type

Consider dogs' coat types when you're thinking about the time you have to care for your dog. Without exception, all dogs shed; some shed more than others, and some dogs' shedding is more troublesome and obvious than others.

Shedding normally occurs when the growth of new hair pushes the old hair out of the follicle. In wild animals, hair grows more as winter approaches and the hours of daylight become shorter. This gives the animal its thick protective coat. Then, when days become longer in the spring, the follicles grow new summer hair that pushes the winter hair out. It's the length of daylight, not the temperature, that normally causes an animal's new hair to grow and its old hair to be shed. The length of daylight is called the *photoperiod.*

A house dog lives under the same conditions as does its owner. When it gets dark, we turn on the lights, so the photoperiod of the house dog is almost the same in winter and summer; therefore, follicles in the dog's skin continue to grow new hair, which is why house dogs shed all year long.

The kind and amount of hair a dog sheds depends on the type of coat the dog inherits from its parents. There are four basic coat types: long, short, medium, and "poodle."

Most dogs have what is called a double coat. This means that they have two kinds of hair: the outer coat that you see and the undercoat made up of thin, fluffy hair that insulates their bodies from cold. The super-short-coated breeds, like Dobermans and dachshunds, have very little undercoat. When they shed, it's the stiff little hair from the outer coat.

Some other short-coated breeds, such as the Jack Russell terrier and most hounds, have quite a lot of undercoat and a longer outer coat than the Dobe or doxie. They shed both kinds of hair and it's more noticeable on your clothes and the rug, especially if the hair is white.

Among the medium-coated breeds are the shepherd types, the retriever types, and many others. These dogs shed a lot. When you purchase one, get a steel comb and a good vacuum sweeper.

Long-coated breeds include, among others, collies, spaniels, Old English sheepdogs, and Pekingese. Not only do they shed, they also develop mats of hair, especially around the hind legs, the belly, and the neck. Some of these breeds, such as the cocker, are often partly clipped, but this doesn't eliminate much shedding or matting unless they are clipped all over including the legs.

Poodle-coated dogs are sometimes considered to be nonshedding, but this isn't really true. In a dog with this type of coat, the hair follicles have a prolonged growing period, so the hair gets very long before it is shed. This long hair is like a sheep's wool. It can form thick, dense mats that contain both the growing hair and the shed hair. If these dogs aren't trimmed regularly, the mats can become so thick and dense that they actually interfere with the dog's ability to walk normally or even to move its bowels.

A few breeds other than poodles have this kind of coat, such as the Puli and the Irish water spaniel. Poodle coated mixed-breed dogs undoubtedly had one or more ancestors that were poodles. All these dogs need regular trimming. You can do it yourself with a scissors if you want to, but it takes a lot of time. Or you can buy an electric clipper, get a book from the library, and learn to do a better, quicker job.

If you don't to want spend much time or money on your dog's coat, pick one that needs only an occasional brushing, pay a groomer to do it for you, or learn to live with hair on the rug and mats on the dog.

Diet

All healthy dogs need approximately the same diet. The amount varies, of course, according to the size of the eater. Figure that a 60-pound (27 kg.) dog such as a retriever will need to be fed three-quarters to one pound (.3–.45 kg) of good-quality dry dog food a day. Depending on the density of the product, that's four to six measuring cups full. A 10 pound (4.5 kg) Chihuahua-type dog will need less than one-half a cupful a day. This means that a 5 pound (2.3 kg) bag of dogfood will last your retriever type dog less than a week, but will last your tiny dog more than a month. You can check prices of a bag of premium dog food at the grocery store, figure out the price per pound, and decide how much you want to spend.

Breed

Nothing much has been said about choosing a special breed of

A growing dog requires a lot of food.

because a puppy has "papers" doesn't mean that it is healthy, a good representative of its breed, free of inherited defects, or has a good disposition. "Papers" don't necessarily mean that the puppy is worth the price asked for it.

Some humane organizations try to convince the public to buy only mixed breeds by claiming that pedigreed dogs are a mass of hereditary and congenital disease. These people feel that a public that is suspicious of purebreds will buy more shelter dogs. One organization even distributes a booklet listing no fewer than 334 separate diseases found in purebred dogs, and more than 40 diseases in one breed alone! They imply that mixed breed dogs have no inherited problems, which, of course, is not true. The truth is that all dogs inherit whatever their parents' genes contain, good or bad. Since each inherited characteristic is determined by genes from the sire and genes from the dam, if both parents are of the same breed, they are more likely to have the same good genes and the same bad ones. Mixed breeds also have inherited defects, only less frequently. Which is a better pet? Neither purebred nor mixed breed has the advantage. Don't believe everything you read or hear about dog breeds. Every dog, like every person, is an individual. Weigh your circumstances and preferences, look at many dogs and make up your own mind.

dog because more than three-quarters of all dogs at shelters in the United States are mixed breeds. Purebred full-grown dogs are often found at shelters but purebred puppies are rare, so if you insist on a pedigreed puppy, you'll probably have to buy one from a breeder.

There's usually nothing wrong with getting a pedigreed dog. Most purebred dogs are produced by conscientious people who try to breed healthy animals. But remember, really good purebred puppies can cost hundreds of dollars, and, when anything is for sale at a high price, all sorts of unscrupulous people will claim that their product is also worth a high price, even if it isn't. "Purebred" puppies are often the result of mating any two dogs of the same breed with no regard to the quality of the animals. The offspring of these matings will be like their parents, which may be mediocre at best. Just

Chapter Eight
Start Your Search

You know exactly what you want; you have figured the space, time, and money you can devote to the dog; you have compromised where necessary. Now is the time to start searching animal shelters for exactly the right pet. Be determined to get only the perfect pet; if you don't find it the first time, go home without a dog and try another day or at another shelter.

Look at Every Dog

If you've done your homework, you have two lists. The first contains the names, addresses, telephone numbers, and visiting hours of all the animal shelters within your search area. This list may also contain the extras offered by each shelter such as vaccinations and low-cost spay and neuter surgery. The second list is the one you just made containing all the qualities you want in your dog. Now you're ready.

If possible, go to shelters when they are not crowded with lookers. This means going on a weekday, not on the weekend. On a slow day, you'll have a better chance to examine all the dogs and talk with the personnel. Take adult members of your immediate family with you if you can.

You're in luck if the shelter has on its staff a person whose job it is to know the history and temperament of each dog and who can help the prospective buyer select the right one. This person may be called an adoption counselor, an advisor, or by another name, so ask to speak with someone who can help you choose a dog.

If they have such a person, hand over the list and stand there trying to look patient while it is being read. If you're in luck, the adoption counselor will be impressed by your thoroughness and will glance up, smile, and say "Have a look around, while I check the files."

Don't be alarmed when you walk through the kennel door; almost every dog in the place will be barking: "Take me! Take me!" Note all the individuals that might fit your requirements, and write down the cage numbers if there are more than a few.

When you've looked over all the available dogs, question the counselor about the origin of any dog

Looking for a big dog? Here are two shepherds for your selection.

mer owner (which they are not required to release to you), and a brief description of the dog and its habits. Often this information is on a printed card that has items to be circled Yes or No. Housebroken? Good with children? Barks? Had obedience training? Good with cats? Needs to be the only pet? Spayed or neutered? The most important item on each dog's record is why was it relinquished? Read this very carefully.

Reasons for Relinquishing a Dog

Some of the reasons given for relinquishing a dog can easily be a cover-up for a real problem. A common statement is "Moving, can't take dog." Another is "Child allergic." While the former owner may actually be moving, and the child may actually be allergic, it certainly is possible that Mom is "moving" heaven and earth to get rid of the dog, because she's "allergic" to cleaning up its messes.

Another common reason for relinquishing a dog is that it "needs room to run." This is given as the reason for relinquishing large young dogs, often purebreds. It really means that the dog is too rowdy and destructive for the owners to tolerate in the house. Those owners purchased a puppy without consideration of the size it would grow to be and the amount of time and space it would require. When it got to be too much trouble, it went to the shelter.

that seems to come close to fitting your ideal. At shelters where there is no adoption counselor, ask to see all the paperwork they have on each of your choices. All shelters should record the origin of each dog even if it was picked up as a stray. For dogs that were relinquished, the shelter will have the name of the for-

You can easily interpret the meaning of many of the other excuses given by people who want to get rid of a dog. "Doesn't like children" means that it will bite if a child gets near its food or toys. "Nobody home all day" means that the dog tears up furniture and carpeting when left alone. "Hates to be on a chain" means that the former owners tied the dog outside and the neighbors complained about the barking. "Not housebroken," a very common reason, means that the owners left the dog loose in the house, untrained and unconfined. Of course it's not housebroken. Without being taught, there's no way a dog can know what it means to be housebroken. None of these excuses nor the many others that are given are necessarily a reason to reject a dog. All they are is an indication that the dog might have a problem. It is up to you to decide if you want that particular dog enough to solve any problems it might have.

Listen to the shelter personnel and read all the cards, but make up your own mind. Everyone who relinquishes a dog would like to think it will get a good home, and many of them are willing to stretch the truth to insure that it does. Almost all people who work at shelters are dog lovers, and they want you to take one of their dogs, so they might not tell you everything you need to know. Look at every prospect with an open mind.

Behavior of Dogs in Cages

Watch the cage behavior of each dog that interests you. Confinement

This dog would love a new home.

in a small wire cage with dozens of dogs in cages nearby, each one barking its head off, is an abnormal situation for any dog. The behavior of a dog in a cage is never normal. Still, you can learn a great many things from their actions.

When a person approaches a caged dog, the dog can react in one of several ways. A fearful dog cowers in the back of the cage, as far from the person as it can get. It trembles in terror like a wild animal. It is likely to show its teeth and snap at any hand that approaches it. It can leap around the back of the cage if an attempt is made to leash it. Dogs that act like this often have had little or no contact with people, and they are terrified. Don't be fooled into thinking that the poor dog must have been abused, and you can show it that you're a good guy. This dog is acting from fear, but not the fear of a beating. It is the fear of the unknown, the fear of a wild animal for a human being.

The average shelter dog looks at a person approaching its cage as a potential friend. Most of them will come to the front of the cage, tail wagging, hoping for human touch. They might bark a little to attract attention. Timid dogs, but not those crazed by fear, will sit or stand and look out at anyone approaching but without coming to the front of the cage. Some perfectly nice dogs won't even get up to see who's there. These dogs have a very reserved nature and usually are not friendly to strangers. They will be happy if you speak to them, and be your friend once you get acquainted, so don't cross a dog off your list just because it doesn't leap up to greet you—it might be just what you want.

The dog that whirls around in its cage, barking frantically and jumping off the bars is usually one that is overanxious for a human friend. Dogs like this are very active and can become playful and responsive pets for someone who takes the time to train them.

Large dogs that leap toward the front of the cage and bark can be quite intimidating, but usually they aren't being vicious; they just want to escape. Some dogs that act that way will be dominant/aggressive; (see pages 50 and 56) but some will not. If you like the looks of a dog that acts that way, ask to see it out of the cage.

A very few dogs will snarl with lips drawn back, hair bristling on their shoulders, when anyone approaches. Even fewer will attack the wires of the cage with their teeth. Such dogs are expressing their resentment and frustration at being caged. Even if you want a guard dog, it's best to avoid these dogs as they have aggressive personalities and hard to train.

Examine the Best Prospects

Ask for a place where you can take each prospect away from the noise and excitement of the kennel. Have the shelter people bring out each of them one at a time so you can see how each dog reacts.

Remember, the dog is in a strange place. It has been confined in a cage or run. It has heard dozens of other dogs barking constantly. The dog doesn't know what's going on, and it will be frightened and confused. You have to make allowances for this when you form an opinion of each one.

You should also make allowances for the fact that the dog has been in a kennel and may be dirty, smelly, and matted. These problems are of no importance; they can be fixed with one grooming session.

Many dogs will greet you like a long-lost friend. They're so glad to be out of the cage and in human company that they'll jump all over you. If they're too active, forgive them. They'll calm down after a couple of days, and you can teach them how to behave.

Be Cautious with Strange Dogs

It's very unlikely that an adoption counselor will bring out a dog that's a biter, but beware! Many dogs—puppies and adults alike—are shy of strangers. This alone is not a cause to reject them. Stand or sit quietly for a few minutes, holding the leash, and see if the dog comes to you for a sniff. If it does, offer your hand, and then stroke its head a little. Most scared-to-death shelter dogs are anxious to make up to any friendly person. These dogs often become the most devoted and loyal pets as soon as they feel secure; however, unless you're an experienced dog trainer, you don't want to buy a fear-biter or an aggressive animal.

Puppies that have not been handled can be very fearful and may even squeal and try to snap when they're picked up. If the puppy is very young, if you really like it, and you don't have children, buy it anyway. A few days of gentle treatment and a few meals from your hand will teach it that people are okay. Of course, never get a puppy like this for children, and if the pup is more than three or four months old, don't get it at all unless you want to spend a lot of time working with it. Chapter 10 will show you how to estimate the age of a puppy so you don't have to depend on a shelter employee's guess.

A Chihuahua mix or a Maltese mix can be yours to love.

Dominant-Aggressive Dogs

The dominant-aggressive dog is an animal to avoid. A lot of people think they want an aggressive dog and they are proud to have a big, protective, even vicious animal to guard their property or their car. These people learn how bad an idea this is when their own dog bites them! A dog that regards itself as the boss will bite anyone who gets in its way, and this includes the hand that feeds it.

Not all dominant dogs are big, and not all are males. They are usually full-grown, but not always. If a small puppy shows dominant traits, it can be easily retrained as is explained in Chapter 10, but to retrain an adult dominant dog is difficult, uncertain, and sometimes dangerous.

You might not be able to spot the dominant dog at first. It is likely to come out of the kennel wagging its tail, and may even jump up on you and lick your hand. It won't act afraid or try to slink away from your touch; in fact, some dominant dogs only show dominance in certain circumstances, such as when someone approaches their food or toys, and this can be difficult or impossible to detect in a shelter situation. It is the overtly dominant individual that the buyer should reject without a second thought.

A really dominant dog approaches strangers as though it is in charge. It stands up straight on its legs. The hair bristles on its shoulders. Its ears prick forward. It growls low in its throat. Instinctively, you're afraid to reach for it. This dog is likely to "make up" to you in a few minutes, but if you take it home, it will express its dominant personality whenever you do something it doesn't like, and eventually you'll be bitten. It's no fun to own a dog that you're afraid of when it has a toy or a bowl of food. It's no fun to own a dog that snarls or grabs your pants leg when you walk past its bed. It's worse to have your children terrorized by their own pet. So, if a shelter worker brings out any dog that stands stiff-legged and growls, wave it away. There are plenty more to choose from.

The Touching Test

No dog should resent gentle handling, even by a stranger, but many of them do. Try stroking the dog gently on the head, then the neck, then the back. Do this carefully and slowly, while someone else holds the leash so the dog can't turn and bite you. Press down on the dog's shoulders, then on its rear end. Do this several times. A dominant dog won't tolerate anyone, much less a stranger, pushing it around.

Stroke the dog's shoulders and flanks. The places a dog least likes to have handled are its feet, especially its front feet. A dog that is afraid of having its shoulders and flanks stroked and its feet touched will jerk away or try to squirm out of reach. Depending on how strong its avoidance behavior, the frightened dog may be okay when it gets to know you, but the dog that growls, snaps, or gets hysterical at your touch is either dominant or a fear-biter, and you don't want it.

The "Sit" Test

If the dog doesn't resent your handling of its back and legs, you might try the "Sit" test. This is done exactly the same way an obedience trainer starts to teach the command "Sit," but the purpose is different. At this time, you don't care if the dog learns anything; you just want to see its reaction to handling. To perform the "Sit" test, hold the leash just behind the dog's head, pull up on it, and at the same time press its hips down into a sitting position with your other hand. The dog that growls or reaches for your hand when you make it sit may be dominant or aggressive. The dog that happily wiggles around to avoid sitting isn't being aggressive. It just doesn't understand the meaning of your actions, and it is not resenting your touch.

A large number of shelter dogs, even in that unusual and scary environment and even with a stranger, will roll over on their backs to have their stomach rubbed and will submit to almost any kind of handling without protest. If you find one of these with most of the qualities on your list, take out your money. That's your dog.

The Importance of Age

People often are too concerned with the age of a dog. Unless you've decided to get a puppy, in which case its age can be estimated fairly accurately, or unless your dog was relinquished to the shelter by its former owner and the age is recorded, a dog's true age is anybody's guess. Shelter personnel and former owners don't always tell the truth because they want to make each dog seem as desirable as possible. Young dogs are considered to be more in demand because they are supposed to be over the puppy stage and still have most of their lives ahead of them. The fact is that all dogs from six months to about two years old are considered adolescents. Some of them will behave like mature dogs and some of them will act like puppies that have the size and strength of adults. You may be happier and more successful with an older dog.

Many people avoid buying "old" dogs, which could mean any dog from five to ten years old. This can be a major mistake. If you want a loyal, devoted, enjoyable pet and you turn down a dog just because it's "too old," you deprive yourself of years of pleasure. Don't buy the wrong dog just because it's young, and don't overlook the right one because it's a few years older

The Teeth of a Mature Dog

The teeth often are used to estimate an adult dog's age, but the teeth of a mature dog don't tell very much. It's a little easier with a young animal. A dog from eight months to one year old will have all its permanent teeth in place and fully erupted.

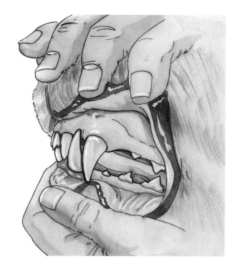

At that age, the teeth should be white and free of tartar at the gum-line. The incisors, those little teeth in front, should have irregular rough edges. After a few years, tartar starts to form on the molar teeth, and then on the canines, or fangs. The edges of the incisors are worn smooth, and

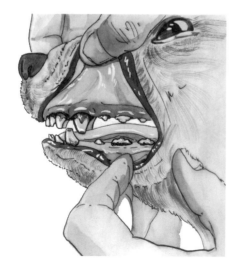

The teeth of an old dog show wear, tartar, and breakage.

signs of wear might appear on the molars.

Heredity and environment play a larger part in the condition of a dog's teeth than age alone. Some dogs inherit a tendency to have poor or misaligned teeth that will fall out or show wear early in life. Some dogs have been fed a diet that promotes the formation of dental tartar and gum disease. On the other hand, some dogs, like some people, inherit perfect teeth that look healthy for many years. Dogs that have had a proper diet and superior dental care may have teeth that look far younger than those of dogs whose teeth were neglected. Once in a while, you might find a young dog that has chewed on rocks or the wires of a chain-link fence; its teeth will be badly worn and might look old even though there might be little tartar on them. Calculating the age of a dog from its teeth is a guess at best. All that can be determined is that a dog is young (under two years), middle-aged (three to seven years old), or probably over seven or eight.

The Eyes

Another way to try to detect an old dog is by its eyes. As dogs and people get older, the lenses of their eyes undergo changes. This is called *cataract* formation in both species. Just as in people, cataracts occur most often in the older individual. A very old dog is likely to have a cloudy look deep in its eyes. In almost all cases, both eyes will look the same. This is not to be confused with a gray or opaque *cornea,* which is the outer surface of the eye. This condition is usually due to injury or disease.

Gray Hair

A dog with gray around the nose and mouth is often mistakenly thought to be old. Graying of hair, both in humans and dogs, is only partly age-dependent. Everyone knows young people with gray streaks, and everyone knows someone's grandpa with a whole head of dark hair. Many dogs get gray around the face and muzzle as they age but just as many never get gray at all. Some dogs are born with white markings on their chins or faces that can resemble the gray hairs on the face of an aging dog. In dogs, gray hair around the face is not a reliable indication of old age.

The conclusion is that there is no easy method of determining the age of any dog over seven months. The best thing to do is to forget it! Get the right dog regardless of its age.

Neutered or Spayed?

How can you tell if a dog is spayed or neutered? You can assume that puppies from relinquished or abandoned litters are not, and young adult dogs at shelters usually are not because nobody cared enough about them to have it done. But if you're considering an older dog, it may have already had surgery and nobody knows it, especially if the dog was a stray. If it was relinquished, the former owner might even have claimed that a female dog had been spayed when in fact it had not been.

Males

It's usually easy to tell if a male dog has been *neutered,* the lay person's term for the surgical removal of the testicles. The medical term for this is *castration.* Normal uncastrated male dogs have two testicles located in the scrotum. You can see them and feel them. A dog with no testicles cannot always be assumed to have been surgically neutered because some dogs have testicles that never descended from their abdominal cavity into their scrotum. These dogs are called *cryptorchids,* a term that means "hidden testicles" in Greek. Dogs with only one testicle descended into the scrotum are called *monorchids,* which means "one hidden testicle." Unless both testicles are surgically removed, cryptorchids and monorchids will act in every way like a dog that has not been neutered.

If you find a mature dog with only one testicle, the dog is sure to be a monorchid, because no veterinarian normally removes only one testicle and leaves the other. The missing testicle is somewhere in the dog's body, and in order for the dog to be neutered, that testicle must be found and removed along with the other one.

If you can't see or feel any testicles, the dog usually has been surgically neutered. Cryptorchids are relatively rare. It can be difficult to detect a real cryptorchid, but a veterinarian often can feel the testicles if they are present in the dog's abdomen or flank area. The surgery to castrate monorchid and cryptorchid dogs can be much more difficult than the surgery to castrate normal ones, so it will be more expensive. This may be a consideration in choosing a dog at a shelter, because if the shelter doesn't have subsidized spays and neuters, you will have to pay the entire cost of the surgery yourself.

Females

There is a more difficult problem with the female dog. There are nothing like testicles to see or feel, and the ovaries and uterus that are surgically removed are deep within the body. This surgery is called an *ovariohysterectomy,* or a "spay." Female dogs that have not been spayed have fertile periods every five to seven months on the average. Veterinarians call these *estrus* periods; laymen call them *heat.* In between these periods, females that are not spayed look the same as those that are spayed, with a few exceptions.

When a female dog has an estrus period, hormones cause enlargement of the external genitals, called the *vulva,* which gets smaller again when the female dog goes out of heat. The dog's nipples and mammary glands also enlarge during heat periods, pregnancy, and lactation. After several heat periods, even if the dog has never been pregnant, the vulva, nipples, and mammary glands never return to quite the same small size they were before puberty. A female dog over two years old that has a juvenile vulva and small nipples can safely be assumed to have been spayed before her first heat. A female with a larger vulva and nipples certainly could have been spayed when she was older, and even after she has had one or more pregnancies.

Many spayed dogs have a surgical scar located on the midline of the abdomen below the navel. The more recent the surgery, the more obvious the scar; an old scar can be nearly invisible. The dog that was spayed in puppyhood will have a smaller and fainter scar than one spayed in adulthood. The scar will be from one-half to three or four inches long, depending on the age and condition of the patient and the technique of the surgeon. Sometimes the scar can be felt as a bumpy line where the sutures were placed, but with modern surgical technique, this evidence is not infallible.

The scar appears as a thin white line. It is covered with hair and usually shows only when the dog's abdomen is shaved. Every veterinary surgeon has anesthetized and prepared dogs for surgery, only to find that the dogs have already been spayed as evidenced by the surgical scar. Very rarely will the surgical scar be from abdominal surgery other than an ovariohysterectomy.

If there is any question that a female dog has been spayed you can always wait a few months to see if she comes in heat, but this will rarely be necessary. Your veterinarian often will be able to find a surgical scar if she's had surgery.

Tattoos on Surgically Altered Dogs

In 1980 the American Veterinary Medical Association recommended that spayed and neutered animals be identified by a tattoo placed on the abdominal or inguinal area while they are still under anesthesia. The recommended tattoos look like the circle-with-a-cross-below-it female symbol or the circle-with-an-arrow-through-it male symbol, but with an "X" through the circle, symbolizing that the animal is no longer able to reproduce. Unfortunately, the practice never became popular, although the application of the tattoo is quick and easy. An even simpler method of identifying animals that have had surgery has been proposed: If the newly-closed incision is rubbed with sterile tattoo ink, it will become dark and will be visible for the life of the animal. If this simple procedure were to become widespread, shelters could tell with assurance which dogs had already had surgery.

Good Luck!

You may have searched at four or five shelters. You may have been to each one a couple of times. Finally

Tattoos applied to the abdomen make it easy to detect a surgically-altered dog. The "male" and "female" signs are crossed-out to signify that the dog is neutered or spayed. Alternately, if the surgeon elects to apply tattoo ink to the new incision, the scar will be visible for the life of the dog.

you found the perfect animal, one that has most of the traits you want and no problems that you can't deal with. You're ready to start your lives together.

But finding the right dog is just the beginning. Puppy or adult, the dog's previous life has been in a different world than yours. Your relationship will not be perfect until each of you learns to understand the other. That won't take long. Together, you can do it.

Chapter Nine
Will It Bite?

All dogs can bite. When you chose your shelter dog, your main concern was to pick one that won't. It's easy to spot a dog that is a *bad* biter, but not so easy to detect one that might bite only under certain conditions.

Millions of dogs bite millions of people every year. Some dogs bite strangers; some bite their owners or members of their owners' families; some dogs bite anyone who comes within their reach.

Reasons that Dogs Bite People

Dominance-Aggression

The term, *dominance-aggression* refers to a dog that views itself as the boss and will bite or threaten to bite in order to retain its position. Very few dogs are born dominant-aggressive, although some dogs have a greater genetic tendency toward that behavior. Even these dogs have to learn to be dominant. All healthy puppies try to grab food and toys, and to jump up on people and on each other. They growl and bite in aggressive play. The myth that a puppy will be better adjusted if it remains with its litter for the first eight or nine weeks of its life apparently is based on the theory that the pup will have been taught to not be dominant by the competition of its littermates. If this is so, the runt would be the best choice to own, as the "pick of the litter" would come with a built-in dominant personality. Obviously, this is not true. A dog learns to be dominant toward humans only when its aggressive actions against humans go unchallenged.

Large dogs are not the only ones to try to act dominant; smaller breed dogs try to assume a dominant role as well. Even though some dogs inherit a greater tendency to be dominant than others, dominance-aggression is a characteristic of individual dogs, not always of any particular breed or type. When you get a shelter dog, you have no way of knowing what its parents were like, so you must be alert for signs of aggressive behavior. If you buy a puppy, it's easy for you to influence it as it matures and thus prevent dominance-aggression from developing. Before you buy an adult dog, you can observe it for signs of aggression toward humans and, therefore, you can avoid dogs with these traits. If you find out later that your dog has inherited or is developing some dominant tendencies, you can correct these tendencies before any harm is done.

The question is often asked: Can you really control aggressive behavior in a dog? If it is a puppy, the answer is an unequivocal *Yes*. It might take quite a lot of time and effort, but the answer is still *Yes*—if you do it correctly and you're willing to go to the considerable trouble it will require. An aggressive older dog can have its attitude changed by training, but often the only person who will be completely safe with the dog will be the trainer.

Dogs reach social maturity at eighteen months to two years of age, but some puppies show dominant behavior much younger than that. Aggression can start at any age. A few puppies as young as four weeks old will growl aggressively over food. Their owners may think it's amusing that such a small puppy would challenge them, but it's not so funny when the puppy gets big enough to really bite them. Most dogs that become dominant don't start to show aggression toward people until they're at least seven or eight months old. At that age they may begin to growl at anyone who approaches their food or toys. If not corrected, the aggression gets worse as the dog gets older.

Dominant-aggressive dogs may act dominant only under certain circumstances, or they may act that way most of the time. Some dominant dogs resist being touched and will bite if anyone even tries to attach their leash. Grooming them is out of the question. At mealtime, the owner drops the dish and gets out of the way.

Here is a typical situation: The young dog begins to growl whenever someone approaches its food; next it bites the child that picks up its toy, then it grabs the pants leg of a person walking past its bed. By this time, everyone in the family is intimidated by the dog that was supposed to be their best friend. They're afraid of it, disappointed in it, and offended that an animal on which they lavished so much love and care should be willing, even anxious, to cause them pain. Everyone cries when the decision is made to get rid of the dog. What went wrong with their cute little pup?

Actually, nothing went wrong with the puppy; something went wrong with its owners. Dogs' ancestors lived in packs and domestic dogs still have a pack mentality. Every pack has a leader, the biggest and toughest member. The leader can bite any other pack member without fear of reprisal. Because the members of the disappointed family had allowed the pup to become the leader of their pack, the dog had no inhibitions against biting them to enforce its leadership. The dog considered itself to be the alpha, the boss. This particular dog was not genetically dominant, but it had learned that it could successfully bully its human pack members by acting aggressive when its status was challenged.

Dogs are very sensitive to humans' behavior toward one another. Very commonly a dog acts aggressive toward some members of the family and submissive toward the member who is the family's actual alpha. "He only obeys my husband. The children can't do a thing with him," is a not uncommon complaint. The dog has established itself as second-in-command, higher on the social scale than women and children, but lower than the man in the household.

The domestic dog, *Canis familiaris,* has been selected for thousands of years for traits that make it able to live in the society of humans. Dogs that inherit true dominant-aggressive behavior are rare; however, more than 80 percent of these genetically aggressive dogs are males. This certainly doesn't mean that more than 80 percent of male dogs are aggressive. Most male dogs don't have an aggressive bone in their bodies.

Contrary to old wives' tales, neutering won't cure aggressive male dogs. Even early neutering won't prevent this condition from developing. A combination of early neutering and early training will effect a

change in these dogs' attitudes, but some dominant-aggressive behavior may still surface as the dog reaches social maturity.

When dominant-aggressive male dogs are neutered, their behavior is altered to the extent that their episodes of dominance are of shorter duration and are less easily provoked than those of dogs that are not neutered, but they will still be aggressive. These dogs act this way because of two factors: They have a genetic tendency toward dominance, and they have learned that their dominant behavior is to their advantage—they get their own way. They are the Boss.

Puppy Training to Prevent Aggression

Human child psychologists give this advice to parents of aggressive children: Be consistent with discipline; don't allow inappropriate aggressive behavior; don't tease your children; don't roughhouse with them and do give them other outlets for physical activity. Dog "parents" should do the same. Since dominance-aggression is at least a partly learned behavior, owners can unwittingly train their dogs to bite the hand that feeds them. There are many ways to teach your puppy never to bite you.

The Fear-Biter

Dogs bite to protect themselves when they feel threatened. Some puppies and adult dogs are so terrified of any person or new situation that they will make valiant efforts to get away, and will bite fiercely if they can't escape. Many dogs that bite children aren't used to being around them and are afraid of them. Children aren't like adults in a dog's eyes. They are smaller and they act differently when they run around and they yell. Dogs often are frightened by these strange creatures and bite to defend themselves.

Many very good watchdogs act out of fear alone. They sound the alarm by barking loudly at anyone who approaches and at any unfamiliar sound. Such dogs are very effective as early warning systems. Their owners are never caught unaware when a stranger approaches, and since the fearfully barking dog retreats from perceived danger, the owners never find themselves at the wrong end of a lawsuit because their dog bit someone.

Fear-biters are dangerous dogs. Dominant-aggressive dogs often started out as frightened puppies; when they reacted to handling by trying to bite, their human pack members left them alone. The puppy thus escaped the fearful situation and learned that biting was a good defense. Soon biting becomes the puppy's offense. When the four-month-old St. Bernard puppy that weighs 40 pounds (18 kg) bites from fear, the owner may be afraid to discipline it. By the time it weighs 150 pounds (68 kg) it's a dangerous dog. The little Chihuahua puppy that runs under the bed to avoid capture learns to bite the hand that reaches

Teach Your Puppy Never to Bite

1. Don't be afraid to approach the pup's food and toys. If your puppy picks up the wrong object, take it away as quickly and gently as you can.
2. If the pup ever growls or bares its teeth at you, don't back away from it! Hold it firmly by the scruff of its neck and tell it: "No!"
3. Never encourage rough and violent play. Never play "tug-of-war" with your dog. If you play rough, your dog will learn to be violent and grab, pull, and snarl at you. When you let go, the dog will learn that by grabbing and snarling, it can "win."
4. Never tease your dog by playing "keep-away" with a favorite toy. Never hold an object just out of the dog's reach and let it jump frantically and snap at empty air. If you do, it'll learn to jump on you and bite.
5. Most important, when you come home to find that your dog has done something wrong, *never* scream and swing a rolled-up newspaper or a yardstick at it. Never punish your dog unless you catch it in the act, because it won't understand the meaning of the punishment.

for it. Soon it bites anyone who tries to touch it.

Terrified dogs can be unpredictable biters and hard to control. If they're frightened badly enough, they'll bite even their owners from blind fear.

Territorial Aggression

The "guard-dog instinct" is a very powerful force in the canine mind. This strongly-inherited trait is called *territorial aggression.* Dogs' wild ancestors defended their own areas from all intruders, and modern dogs still demonstrate the same behavior. A dog showing strong territorial aggression is very effective in keeping strangers off its owner's property.

The true guard dog threatens strangers only on its home territory, which commonly includes its house, its yard, and its car. Guard dogs in places like factories and auto yards ward off and deter thieves. The guard dog doesn't bite its owners, but it may attack anyone that it perceives as a menace to its owners, as well as those it perceives as a menace to its owners' property. A really good guard dog will not bite when it isn't at home and when its owner isn't threatened. In other words, a good guard dog isn't aggressive when there's nothing to guard.

A *watchdog* is different from a guard dog. A guard dog defends property by first challenging, then attacking trespassers. A watchdog merely announces the presence of unauthorized persons by barking. A watchdog can sound the alarm from territorial instinct or from fear of strangers and the results are the same. The owners are warned if anyone approaches. Small terriers and even the toy breeds have keen hearing and are alert little watchdogs; nobody can sneak up on them. However, the difference between a guard dog and a watchdog is not readily apparent to trespassers since they don't know if the barking dog will retreat or attack. Before you decide on a guard dog, consider whether a watchdog would better suit your purposes. Only nuisance lawsuits are filed over barking dogs, but expensive damage lawsuits are common over those that bite.

Prey Aggression

A seldom-recognized reason that dogs bite children is *prey aggression.* The dogs' wild ancestors were hunters. They had to capture and kill other animals to live. It is likely that dogs that attack infants and small children don't even realize that these are humans. They consider them to be prey species, just as they might consider rabbits or cats. Even though dogs no longer have to kill to eat, their instinctive behavior is to grab and bite something that looks or acts like food. This is especially true if the victim acts like "prey" by screaming or running.

Maternal Instinct

Maternal instinct causes a mother dog with puppies to guard her litter. Wild dogs helped insure survival of their offspring by protecting them from harm, and the behavior remains strong in our domestic canines. Although many mother dogs are happy to allow their pups to be handled, maternal instinct is so strong that even owners should exercise caution with a new mother.

Protect Yourself

You know your own dog. If it's dominant-aggressive, you know under which situations it will bite to assert its status, so you can avoid these situations or you can retrain it not to bite you. You can keep your own dog away from visitors if it's likely to be aggressive toward them.

Someone else's dog is a different story. No matter how much you love dogs and no matter how much experience you've had with them, there are circumstances in which you will be bitten unless you use caution.

Consider the Following Points:

- A dog in its own yard will often bark furiously and back up, but don't trust it—it may take a piece out of your leg the minute you step onto the property. The smart action would be to shout or blow your horn until the owner arrives. And don't just walk into a dog-owning relative's house unannounced. Your sister's dog can bite you just as hard as a stranger's.

- A guard dog in a car often means business. Even a 15-pound terrier can act as though it has 10 pounds of teeth, so don't challenge it. Police often consider a dog in a car to be a better deterrent to crime than another person.

- Loose dogs away from their own property rarely attack people unless they have misdirected territorial aggression or consider the people to be prey. Loose dogs are much more likely to attack children. Teach your child never to run or scream when a strange dog comes near, as this behavior triggers dogs' instinct to chase and attack. The dog is more likely to ignore a child who stands still and keeps quiet.

- Dogs' ancestors hunted in packs; they cooperated with each other in bringing down their prey. Loose dogs even in pairs are more dangerous than single ones, so beware!

- An unfriendly or frightened stray dog will avoid people, but will bite if it's cornered. If you try to catch a stray, don't grab for it. Try slipping a noose made from a rope or leash over its head.

- Anyone who tries to separate fighting dogs risks being bitten. All dogs in a dogfight will bite blindly out of fear and aggression, and will hurt anyone who gets in the way. A dog that is attacking another animal or a person might turn its attack toward anyone who tries to help the victim. Don't wade into a battle unaware of the consequences to yourself.

- Injured dogs, dogs in pain, and dogs entangled in ropes or in their collars will bite every time. The dog in great fear or pain can't realize that you're trying to help it. Never try to rescue a dog hit by a car without taking appropriate precautions, or you'll get chomped. If possible, it's best to call trained personnel like animal wardens to deal with accident victims.

Pit Bulldogs

The English bulldog originated in Great Britain in the 1600s as a participant in the "sport" of bull baiting, which is how they received the name, "bulldog." The original English bulldogs looked and acted nothing like their modern counterparts. When bull baiting was eliminated, some of the dogs of the original type became the foundation of the breeds used in dogfighting. Dogfights were conducted in pits in much the same way as human boxing is conducted in rings, hence the name "pit bulldog." Dogfighting is illegal everywhere in the United States, but there is no doubt that it is conducted in secret in many areas.

The American Kennel Club, the registering body for the majority of purebred dogs in the United States, does not recognize the pit bulldog as a breed. The American Staffordshire terrier is the closest AKC breed to the pit bull in appearance, but it is not a fighting breed. The United Kennel Club, also a dog registering association in the United States, recognizes and registers a pit bulldog and has classes for the breed in UKC dog shows.

The pit bulldog has been selectively bred for generations for its aggressiveness toward other dogs. A dog this aggressive will be more likely to attack other living things, and this includes humans. Real pit bulldogs are a short-haired stocky dog that are usually heavier than 60 pounds (27 kg) and equipped with powerful jaws and an inherent determination to bite and rip and tear and hang on. They can do a lot of damage; they can kill another dog, or even a person.

In some localities, the possession of pit bulldogs is forbidden or regulated by law, but there is great controversy about the enactment and enforcement of these laws. Many dogs of mixed breeding have the appearance of pit bulls but none of their disposition. Many purebred pit bulls are no longer bred for fighting and are no more likely to attack humans or other dogs than are dogs of any other breed. Furthermore, many individual dogs that bear no resemblance whatever to pit bulldogs are aggressive and dangerous.

Since the breed of a dog alone is not the determination of its character, laws that discriminate against any particular breed are often successfully challenged as unconstitutional. Laws that impose strict liability and enforce severe penalties for owners whose dogs run at large are appropriate to deal with the "dangerous dog" problem. Such laws serve to discourage the possession of biting dogs and to encourage the careful confinement of those that are kept.

Almost all humane societies refuse to sell any dog that exhibits severe aggressive behavior, and all shelters are prohibited by law from offering for sale to the public any animal that has been impounded for biting. When you buy a dog from a shelter, it is very unlikely that you will unknowingly purchase anything like a pit bulldog.

Wolves and Wolf-Dog Crosses

The wolf is considered to be a beautiful, noble, and valuable animal. Undoubtedly this is correct when the animal is in the right environment. But the wolf is not a domestic animal. The wolf is a wild animal. It *never* can be a pet.

The genetic similarity of the wolf and the dog is proven by the fact that the wolf, *Canis lupus* and the dog, *Canis familiaris* can and do breed and produce fertile offspring, but in the wild, they would seldom if ever do so. Wild wolves are extremely hostile to domestic dogs. They'd have them for lunch, not for mates.

Unfortunately, some people decided that crosses between wolves and dogs would produce a superior animal: the majestic appearance and great strength of the wolf with the domestic behavior of the dog. These crosses are easy to obtain because captive wolves will mate with dogs, but the resulting hybrid animals are nothing but tragedies.

Wolf-dogs do not act like dog-dogs. Wolf-crosses get part of their genetic makeup, and thus part of their genes for behavior, from the wolf. The wolf has not been selected for thousands of years for characteristics that can live with man. Nature has selected for the wolf the traits that ensure its survival in the wild: aggression, caution, suspicion, self-protection; none of the traits we want in our dogs.

Inherited wolf behavior is dominant to inherited dog behavior. The pups from a wolf-dog cross, even if they are hand raised by humans, will develop wolflike characteristics. They act like wild animals. They are extremely shy. They bite viciously to protect themselves. They are unable to be housebroken and are all but untrainable. They're fearful, dirty, wild, dangerous, and unhappy. Even those that are "only" one-quarter wolf cannot be trusted to be pets.

An occasional animal is seen that acts like a domestic dog but that the owner claims is "part wolf." Don't be fooled—there is no clear-cut anatomical way to tell for sure if an animal really has any wolf blood in it. The friendly, tame "part wolf" probably has no actual wolf blood in its make-up. The nice "wolf-dog" is probably a fraud. It's likely to be a nice mixture of German shepherd and collie.

Chapter Ten
Puppies, Puppies, Puppies

What's the difference between a puppy and a dog? Only a few months, but these are the formative months of the animal's life.

All puppies are cute. All puppies are irresistible. This statement is true—most of the time. But some puppies are skinny, dirty, frightened, or sick. Shelters have both kinds. Both kinds deserve a chance to live.

Almost all puppies at shelters are from unwanted, unplanned litters. They are the sad results of irresponsible owners who allow their female dogs to mate with whatever male comes along. The saddest part is that these owners are able to shirk their responsibility by dumping the pups at an animal shelter, where it becomes the shelter's job to find them homes or put them to death.

To a dog lover, the attitude of some owners is hard to believe: "Uh-oh, Lady's pregnant again. Well, after the children play with the pups for a couple of weeks, I'll just drop them off at the shelter the way I did her last litter. They'll find them good homes." Even worse: "I'll just leave the pups out in the country.

Somebody will take care of them." The truth is that even though shelters sell many puppies, they are forced to euthanize many more, as there simply aren't enough homes for them all. Unless the puppies that are abandoned "out in the country" are taken to a shelter by some kind person, they starve or freeze to death, are killed by cars or other animals, or die of disease. The lives of unwanted puppies are often very short and very miserable. It is a shame to allow them to be born to such a fate.

A dog is considered to be a puppy until its first birthday. Unlike some animals that breed only in the spring and fall, dogs have pups during all months of the year, so shelters usually have a good selection of puppies to choose from. Many dog owners choose a puppy instead of an older dog because they can "raise it the way I want it," or because "if I raise it with my children, it won't bite them." As previously discussed, this is true only if the owner makes sure that the puppy is properly handled and the children have appropriate supervision.

Early Growth of Puppies

The length of the average dog's pregnancy is 63 days, with a normal variation of three or four days shorter or longer. The birth process in dogs is called *whelping* (*whelp* is an old term for puppy). Wild dog-like animals make a den or nest in a secluded place a few days before whelping. Domestic dogs do the same, seeking out a safe place for their litters. The mother dog instinctively licks the birth membranes off each pup as it is born, then encourages it to nurse.

Puppies are blind and deaf at birth because the tissues of the outer ears and the eyelids are not yet fully developed. They cannot stand, but crawl toward the mother in response to her smell and warmth. The inside corners of puppies' eyes begin to crack open around the fourteenth day of life, and within a day or two, the eyes are completely open. By the time puppies are 17 or 18 days old, they react to light and sound. During their third and fourth week, puppies start to get up on their legs and try to walk. By 28 days, most puppies will be scampering around, although they still will be clumsy. They will be able to eat from a dish if they have to, but normally will nurse for a week or two more. Many unwanted puppies are taken to shelters at this age because it is obvious that they soon will require food and care other than that provided by their mother. Irresponsible owners dump them before

These nursing puppies will soon be eating solid food.

they become a nuisance or an expense.

Nursing puppies that are abandoned at shelters require extra care from the shelter staff. Therefore, many of them are euthanized immediately. Lucky puppies go to a shelter that has staff or volunteers willing to raise them and to offer them for adoption when they are old enough, usually six to eight weeks. A myth prevails that puppies taken away from their mother before the "correct" age will be somehow abnormal. This myth is completely untrue. A puppy removed from its litter at the moment of birth and properly hand-raised will be indistinguishable from littermates raised by the dam by the time the pups are 12 weeks old. If

It is not difficult to raise pups on a bottle, but it takes time.

anything, the hand-raised puppy may be a little more socialized toward humans and have somewhat better physical coordination.

At the age of about five weeks, a puppy becomes very aware of its surroundings. Most five-week-old puppies have not yet had many bad experiences, and most are happy to be handled by any gentle person. Those that have had little or no human contact may be fearful of being touched and may cower, try to escape, or even snap at an approaching hand. If such a puppy is given pleasant association with humans before it is 10 or 12 weeks old, it will soon decide that people are its friends. If the puppy receives no favorable human contact until it is four months of age or older, it probably will remain fearful of people for life.

The adult dog you buy may be housebroken, trained to walk on a leash, and familiar with riding in a car. Your new adult dog may even have been to obedience school. If you choose a puppy, it will be up to you to provide all these experiences for it. A young puppy that has to stay alone all day while its owners are at work can be short-changed by the limited time it gets to learn everything it needs to know.

It is particularly important that your puppy be exposed to the outside world while it is still very young. Pups that never encounter a person other than their owners and that never experience an environment other than their own will be very fearful adult dogs. They might be excessively timid away from home, and they might be terrified of strangers. It is very difficult to alleviate the fears of an adult dog that was raised without contact with the world, but it is easy to teach a puppy to be happy and confident in nearly every situation. Your puppy should have seen a little of virtually everything it will experience in its lifetime by the age of 12 or 14 weeks.

Puppy Education

- Your puppy should go places with you.
- It should ride in the car.
- It should be petted and held by many different people.
- After it has been vaccinated, it should meet other dogs.

- It should be introduced to children.
- It should be taken to different yards and different houses.
- It should learn to go for walks on a leash around the block.

If everyone in your family works or goes to school all day and you simply must get a puppy, you will have to take special precautions to see that its education isn't neglected. Make time for it after work, *every* day. Plan to take it somewhere new at least once every weekend. Ask if your children's teacher will let them bring it to school for show-and-tell. Make sure that your pup grows up to be a happy, well-adjusted dog.

What Will It Look Like?

Because almost all young puppies at shelters are mixed breeds from unwanted litters, you'll never know what their parents were like. What you see in a very young puppy is not necessarily what you'll get when it's a mature dog.

The first thing everyone asks about puppies is: what kind of a dog is that? Shelter staff will give each puppy a description, such as: collie-type, shepherd-type, hound-type, terrier-type, poodle-type. However, in mixed-breed pups even experts can't tell for sure, because puppies of 6 to 16 weeks of age don't always look like the dogs they will become. Some of them are not even the same color they will be

This little cutie is just four weeks old.

at maturity. Black puppies often become at least partly brown when they mature, white puppies may develop spots later. All puppies are born with floppy ears, but some of them have ears that will be erect. A thick-coated puppy may turn out to have long hair, medium hair, or anything in between. Since neither you nor the shelter personnel ever see the parents, each pup's combination of breeds can only be a guess.

How Big Will It Be?

The second question every buyer asks is: How big will it get? This is a guess also, and the idea that a puppy with big feet will be a big dog is just another myth. The final size of a dog is determined only by the genes it received from its sire and dam. Of course, small dogs have small puppies, and big dogs have big puppies, but big dogs' puppies are often smaller for their age than you'd expect them to be. The larger the dog, the more puppies it tends to have in each litter, and if there are many puppies in a litter, each puppy will be smaller at birth than those from a litter in which there are few. Also, if there are many puppies in a litter, more have to compete for their mother's milk, which means that each receives less nourishment and will not be as large at weaning as those from a litter of fewer pups. And if puppies are not fed enough after weaning, they will be smaller than those with adequate nutrition. Such puppies will catch up once they get enough to eat, and all will eventually reach their genetically determined size, but sometimes it's hard to tell if a puppy is small because its parents were small or because it needed more nourishment to grow properly.

Shelter personnel often tell buyers that a pup's adult size will be smaller than it really will be. This is probably more wishful thinking than an attempt to deceive, because they want all their pups to find homes, and small dogs are in greater demand. It's best to have enough information to determine some things for yourself.

Size As Related to Age

By the time a pup has all its permanent teeth at six to seven months of age, it has reached 60 to 70 percent of its adult height at the top of the shoulders. As it matures it will get heavier, but only about 30 percent taller.

When you are able tell a puppy's actual age in weeks, you can make a better estimate of the type and size it's likely to be at maturity. For example, if a shelter worker tells you, "That's as big as it's going to get," and you see that the puppy isn't even four months old, you know that he's wrong. If he says, "It'll get twice that big," and the puppy is already six or seven months old, you know that he's wrong again. Estimating the age of a dog from birth to about eight months of age by its teeth isn't very difficult and you don't have to be a canine dentist to do it. Remember though, you can only make an estimate, and there's quite a lot of variation among puppies.

Determining the Age of a Pup by Its Teeth

Most animals, including dogs and people, have baby teeth and permanent teeth. Dogs' baby teeth, like those of people, are called *deciduous teeth*. These are smaller in size and fewer in number than the dog's final set, or permanent teeth. As with the teeth of children, dogs' teeth erupt at known times and can be used to estimate the age of a puppy.

To simplify the situation, only the teeth in the front of the dog's upper jaw will be used in estimating its age.

At Birth

The newborn puppy has no teeth. By 14 days, when its eyes start to open, the front of its upper jaw feels rough where the deciduous incisors are erupting.

Three to Five Weeks of Age

By three weeks, most puppies have two tiny incisor teeth right in the center of their upper jaw. By four weeks, there are four tiny incisors in the upper jaw, two on the right side and two on the left. Also at about four weeks, the fangs begin to appear as little sharp points. The fangs are called *canine teeth* in a dog, and *cuspids* or *eye teeth* in a human.

By five weeks, the last set of deciduous incisors appear, giving the puppy six little incisor teeth along the front of its upper jaw, with a needle-sharp little canine tooth on each side of the row of incisors.

12 to 16 Weeks of Age

As the puppy gets older, its skull grows. Of course its teeth do not grow, so as with a child, its teeth become farther apart. Between 12 and 14 weeks of age, there are usually noticeable spaces between each of a pup's incisor teeth.

The first deciduous teeth a puppy loses are its central upper incisors, the same teeth that came in first. This happens in most dogs at about 16 weeks of age. The two tiny deciduous teeth fall out, and in their place are the beginnings of their permanent central incisors. These are much larger and whiter than the teeth they have replaced. If you see a puppy with a mouthful of baby teeth, but with two big incisors right

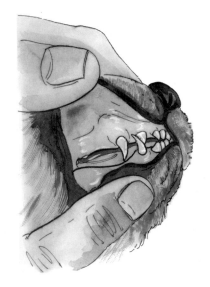

The deciduous teeth of this five-week-old puppy are very sharp!

in the front of its upper jaw, you can say with confidence, "This pup is only about 16 weeks old."

This Australian shepherd puppy will grow to about 45 pounds.

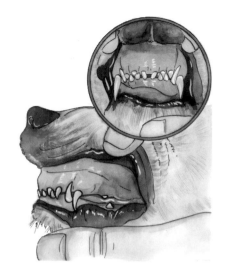

This pup is 14 weeks old. Notice how much farther apart the deciduous teeth have spread.

The most common exception to this rule is the eruption of the permanent teeth in the larger breeds. In shepherd-size or larger dogs, the permanent upper central incisors come in earlier, often at 14 to 15 weeks; in the giant breeds, even sooner, sometimes at 13 weeks.

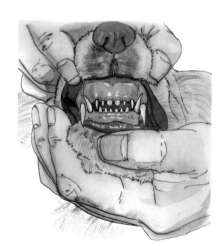

The top central permanent incisors erupt at about 16 weeks. These new teeth are much larger than the ones they replaced.

18 Weeks to Six Months of Age

By four-and-a-half months of age, most dogs have four permanent upper incisors, two on each side. By five months, or 20 weeks, all six of the deciduous upper incisors have been replaced by the permanent ones.

Also at five months, the permanent canine teeth, or fangs, begin to appear in front of the deciduous canine teeth. The deciduous canine teeth remain in place behind the permanent ones for two to four weeks, sometimes longer. When the permanent canines are as long as the deciduous canines, the dog is usually around five to six months of age.

Seven to Eight Months of Age

A dog of seven or eight months will have a whole mouthful of new shiny white teeth. The permanent canines will be fully erupted and will be longer than the deciduous canines, if those are still present. Usually, the deciduous canine teeth have been lost by that time.

Retained Teeth

Retained teeth are those deciduous ones that should have fallen out, but have not. Dogs' baby canines are the teeth most often retained. When present, they are located behind the permanent canines. Retained deciduous incisors are located on top of the permanent ones. Veterinarians recommend that retained teeth be removed because they crowd the permanent teeth and promote decay. Deciduous teeth should be removed

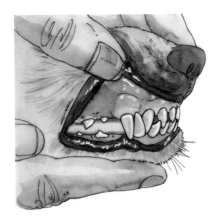

(left) At five months of age, all the permanent teeth are present, but the canines are not yet fully erupted.

(right) This six-month-old pup has a retained deciduous canine tooth behind the permanent one. If the retained tooth is not shed, it should be extracted.

only if they are retained more than a month or two beyond the expected time for them to be lost, as many of these teeth will fall out on their own.

Certain breeds, notably very small dogs such as toy poodles, inherit a tooth and jaw structure that often results in many retained deciduous teeth. These dogs can require more professional dental care than dogs of larger breeds.

Remember, these dates are estimates. Puppies have variations in the age at which they cut teeth.

How to Estimate the Age of a Puppy by Its Teeth

Age	Signs
6 weeks	All tiny deciduous incisors and canines in place.
10 to 14 weeks	The incisors start to move apart, causing spaces to appear between them.
16 weeks	The pair of upper central deciduous incisors are lost and are replaced by the much larger permanent incisors.
18 weeks	The next pair of deciduous incisors are replaced by permanent ones, giving the puppy four big teeth right in the front of its upper jaw.
5 months	The permanent canine teeth, or fangs, appear and all the deciduous incisors are replaced by permanent ones.
6 months	The permanent canine teeth are longer than the deciduous ones; the deciduous canines may be lost by this time.
7 months	All the dog's permanent teeth are in place.

Retained incisors, canines, and some premolars in a six-month old dog. This condition is common in toy breeds, and needs veterinary attention.

Other Important Considerations

Selecting a Shelter Puppy

Many books on dogs emphasize methods of selecting the best puppy from a litter, or describe little "tests" that one can perform to determine if the puppy will or will not be easy to train. For example, in the "follow test" the prospective owner claps his or her hands and calls while walking away from the pup; a good response occurs if the puppy hurries to keep up, a bad response if the puppy ignores the person or goes the other way. The most meaningful of these puppy tests is the one in which the prospective buyer rolls the puppy onto its side or back. Some, but not all, puppies that growl or strongly resist this handling *may* be the ones that have inherited dominant personalities.

Puppies are usually ill at ease in the unfamiliar and frightening atmosphere of a shelter, and won't react in the same manner as they would in a comfortable place, so such tests are of questionable value. In the confusion of a shelter situation, buyers might consider ignoring little puppy tests and buy the pup they like and the one that likes them the best.

Your Responsibility to Your New Puppy

The minute you walk out of the door of the shelter with a puppy in your arms, your responsibility to it begins. The kind of dog you will have depends on every experience you provide for your puppy, so it's up to you to provide only good ones.

If you want your dog to be clean in the house, you must housebreak your puppy (see Chapter 16). If you want it to be friendly, you must see that your puppy gets plenty of human contact. If you want your dog to ride in the car with you, you must get your puppy used to doing it. If you want your dog to be good with children, you must give it carefully supervised experiences with children, and this means the children must be supervised as well as the pup.

On the other hand, if you want your pup to grow into an unruly dog that messes in the house, chews up everything, runs away, bites children, barks all night and attacks the mailman, your job is much easier; all it takes is neglect. If you don't have all the time a puppy requires, get an older dog.

Your Puppy's Continuing Medical Care

Most humane societies' shelters start each puppy on its vaccinations, treat it for internal and external parasites, and set up a written schedule detailing when the pup is due for additional procedures. They will give you a copy of this record when you take your puppy home. In some cases you can take the pup back to the shelter veterinarian; in most cases you'll need to make an appointment with your own veterinarian to continue your pup's immunization and other essential care.

Leash Training

A puppy needs a lot of education. It needs to be acquainted with the human race and the big world out there. It needs to be taken for a run in the park, for a ride in the car, or for a visit to the schoolyard to be petted by all the children. To make this possible, one of the first lessons you should give your pup is how to walk on a leash.

Nothing is easier than to teach a small puppy about a leash, and nothing is more difficult than to try to teach an older dog that has had its early education neglected. For the puppy, it's done in three steps:

1. Fit it with a lightweight plain buckle collar. The collar should be tight enough that it can't slip over the pup's head, and cheap enough to discard when the pup grows. Don't start with too big a collar, and don't buckle it so loose that the puppy can get its lower jaw into it when it tries to chew the collar, or get its foot caught when it scratches at it. It will do both as soon as you buckle on the collar, and it will take a couple of days of wearing it until the pup forgets that the collar is there.

2. When your puppy is used to the collar, attach a lightweight leash or piece of cord to the collar, and let the pup drag it around for a few minutes at a time, once or twice a day. Watch that the leash doesn't become tangled in anything and frighten your puppy. Unlike the collar, you'll take the leash off between training sessions, or the puppy will learn to chew it up.

3. After three or four ten-minute sessions of the puppy dragging the leash around, you'll pick up the end and *coax* the puppy to follow you. Use food, a toy, pat your leg, whatever works to get your puppy to follow while you hold the end of the leash. Don't drag the pup if it doesn't come with you, you'll frighten it and make your job harder. Coax and use little tugs on the leash. If the pup goes the other way, go with it. Soon it will realize that it is connected to you by the leash and it has to go where you go.

That's all there is to it. Your puppy will be leash-trained in three or four days and well on its way to becoming socialized. You are on your way to many years of happy companionship.

Chapter Eleven
Plan Ahead Before You Take Your Dog Home

Today is the big day! You've looked at all the shelters in your area and you've picked out your dog. You know it's the right one, and you anticipate years of happy companionship. But are you prepared to get a good start?

You wouldn't bring a new baby home from the hospital without any preparation, without even buying a crib and some formula. Start right with your new dog, too. Get everything ready and know what you're going to do before you get it from the shelter.

Your New Dog's Quarters

The Safe Space

The most important decision is this: Where you are going to keep the new dog?

If you say, "Why, in the house, of course," you must decide where in the house. Remember, you don't know anything about your new pet except the little information you got

from the shelter. If it is an adult dog, you don't know its habits and behavior. You don't know if it's really housebroken, you don't know if it's destructive, you don't know if it jumps on furniture. If you think the animal will behave perfectly from the start, you might be badly disappointed, because every new dog must be taught to live with you in your household. You can have a dog and also a clean, neat house if you use a Safe Space to keep both your possessions and your dog safe from harm.

Would a sensible owner bring a strange dog into his home and turn it loose without supervision? Not likely. A sensible owner would want to train his or her dog to not be dirty or destructive before it is allowed unlimited freedom in the house. A sensible owner would arrange a Safe Space in which to keep the new dog when no one can be around to supervise it.

This is where the Safe Space comes in. A Safe Space is an escape-proof enclosure for a dog when it is left alone. When you use a

Safe Space, your dog is safe and your property is safe; that's why it's called a *Safe* Space. Without such a Space, your dog is free to mess on the carpet, chew up belongings, jump on the furniture, and bark at the neighbors. An owner can reduce or eliminate the use of the Safe Space once the dog is trained, but every dog should have its own Safe Space at the start, and it should be arranged before the dog comes home from the shelter. Part of the decision you made when you decided on the size of dog you wanted (in Chapter 7) was based on the area you had available to locate the Safe Space.

A cage, a kennel, a pen, a crate—these terms all mean the same thing: a place in which you can lock up the dog where it cannot do damage to your household or to itself. Unfortunately, some people mistakenly equate confinement with cruelty. People tend to feel guilty about confining their dog instead of being confident that they are handling the situation correctly and sensibly.

Unless you bought a young puppy, the very dog you chose for your own might well have been discarded by its former owners because of the lack of a correctly used Safe Space. "It's too active." "It's not housebroken." "It chews things." "It scratches the door." These are reasons given for relinquishing a dog, and none of these reasons exist if a Safe Space is used properly. The dog that is allowed unsupervised freedom in the house

before it is trustworthy often is the dog that gets abandoned at a shelter. You aren't being cruel when you prevent your new animal from damaging your property. You'd be far more cruel if you allowed it to wreck your home, and then when you won't put up with the destruction anymore, you abandoned it to an unknown fate. You can't expect a dog to obey your rules if you haven't taught it those rules. You can't expect a dog to learn those rules in only a few days, or to obey them in your absence. So, when you aren't there, use the dog's Safe Space to keep it out of trouble.

You will read that dogs love to be in their own little dens, but you might observe the opposite. Your dog is not likely to accept confinement happily. It would rather be with you or be free to explore. If it has never been confined, it may whine, bark, and scratch at the door of the Space. Ignore it. It's far better for

This dog's Safe Space is a roomy cage.

your dog to learn to accept confinement than to be without a home. It's far better for your disposition for you to confine the dog when appropriate than to have your house damaged. It's far better for your wallet to buy a dog cage than a new couch or new carpeting.

Size of the Safe Space: For a small or medium-size dog or for a puppy, the Safe Space should be a cage or escape-proof pen; you can buy one or make one yourself. The key words are *escape-proof;* dogs are often very good at getting out of things or getting over things. For very large dogs, you might have to use a fenced-off part of a laundry room or garage. You need to make a space that contains *nothing* that can be destroyed, and *nothing* that can be torn apart and swallowed.

The size of the Safe Space for a puppy should match the size that the dog will need when it's full-grown. You hope your puppy won't need to be confined when it's an adult, but you know there are times that it will need to be while it's growing up. Because of the cost and trouble of setting up an adequate Safe Space, plan to make it big enough so you don't have to enlarge it later. Within only a few months, your puppy will have grown into its adult-size Space.

The size of a dog's permanent Safe Space need not be more than twice the area that the dog needs to lie down and stretch out. Locking a dog in a garage, a laundry room, a bathroom, or any other small room is not the same as providing it with a proper Safe Space because there are things in those places that a dog can chew; there are doors it can scratch, toxic substances it can lick, and plenty of room in which it can mess in garages and laundry rooms. Buy, build, or arrange a secure Safe Space.

This little dog's basket is in its safe space.

The Outside Relief Area

The new dog's outside area is important too. You'll train your dog to eliminate outside unless you are an apartment dweller and get a tiny paper-trained pet. You will want your dog to eliminate in one area so cleanup is easy, therefore, you must select that area ahead of time and teach the dog where it is and what it's for.

At least while you're training it, you will have to walk your dog at intervals on a long leash to its bathroom area. A place on gravel or concrete is a good choice because it's easy to clean up. Try to choose a place close to an outside door and always take the dog out the same door while you're housebreaking it. That's the way to teach a dog to "run to the door" when it wants to go out.

Things Your Dog Will Need

After you've designed and set up your Safe Space and decided where the outside bathroom area will be, you're nearly ready to bring your new dog home. You need to get only a few more items:

Food

Try to get some of the same food your new dog has been eating. Ask what they were feeding at the shelter and continue the same food for a few days. If you need to make changes to another type or brand of food, do it gradually. Resist the urge to give the poor skinny little thing too much food at one time. Overfeeding, particularly a dog that isn't used to a good diet, is the surest way to give your new dog a bad case of diarrhea.

Collar and Leash

A choke chain, small enough that it can't slip over its head, is good for an adult dog until you are sure that it won't try to escape by backing out of a collar. A puppy should have a small, inexpensive buckled collar, fitted tightly enough so that the pup

Every grocery store has a huge selection of dog foods. Read the labels to choose the best one.

can't get its jaw under the collar when it tries to chew on it (see page 73). The fit of a collar must be checked weekly; pups grow but collars do not. Any kind of a leash will do, including a piece of rope, but it should be six feet (1.83 m) or longer. Don't use a chain for a leash as it will hurt your hands when the dog yanks.

Bowls

You can use an old pie pan, or you can use Grandma's best china—the dog won't care. You'll have less of a mess if the dish doesn't tip over easily, and if you leave food or water containers inside the Safe Space, be sure they're not chewable, like plastic. Many a dog has eaten its plastic dish and required surgery to remove the pieces from its intestines.

Bedding

Newspapers are the best to start with, until you find out if the dog will mess in its Space. If it chews and eats blankets, it can get pieces

Take your new puppy home in a secure kennel.

Most dogs would rather ride next to the driver.

Taking It Home in the Car

Your new dog will be excited by finally getting out of a cage at the shelter. Ask the shelter personnel to put it in a run for a few minutes or take it for a nice long walk before you put it in your car. A mess on your car seats is not a good way to start a happy relationship.

If you're getting a puppy or a very small dog, you should have some sort of a carrier to put it in when you take it in the car. A cardboard box with a lid and air holes works fine. This will keep the puppy out of trouble and your car clean. Avoid a struggle: Take the box into the shelter, put the puppy in it, close the lid, then carry it out to your car. Even if you have a friend hold the puppy while you drive, a box will prevent the possibility of a mess in your car or on your friend. Never expect a puppy to sit quietly in a box without a lid. Usually, it will do everything possible to climb out.

Your new adult dog will have to ride with you in the car. It's a good idea to put an old blanket on the seat since the dog has been in a shelter and it probably isn't too clean. Tuck the blanket into the seat so the dog can't kick it loose and get your upholstery dirty.

stuck in its intestines, as with pieces of the plastic dish. Something other than newspapers is needed only in a pen built on concrete, because dogs should not have to lie on a cold concrete floor. A wooden platform for a bed is a good solution, but the edges must be protected to prevent the dog from chewing the wood and swallowing the splinters.

How to Control the Adult Dog in a Car

Here's how a lone person can

control almost *any* dog in almost *any* car:

- Attach a leash or a piece of rope about 4 feet (1.22 m) long to the dog's secure collar. Don't use a chain because it will scratch the paint on your car door.
- Open the right rear door of the car and let the dog get in. If it's never been in a car or if it doesn't like to ride, you may have to boost it in or pick it up and lift it in. If you have a two-door car, put it in on the right side, either behind the front seat or next to you in the passenger's seat. Don't let go of the rope or leash.
- Then simply close the car door on the rope, allowing the dog enough rope on the inside to move around a little, but not enough to get into trouble or to jump on you.
- Leave the rest of the rope or leash sticking outside of the car on the handle side of the door. The dog is secured by the short length you've allowed it inside the car.

Never tie a dog anyplace where there is the slightest possibility it could hang itself. Always keep the window up on the right side, and have the rope short enough so the dog can't try to jump into the back seat.

Most car doors don't fit tightly enough to keep an active dog from pulling too much rope into the car. To prevent this, tie a big knot in the rope or leash close to the door on the outside. The knot will keep the rope from being pulled into the car.

- With the dog controlled by the rope closed in the door on the right side

of the car, you are able to open the driver's side door and get in without allowing the dog to jump out. It can't move beyond the length of its rope inside the car, so you can drive without interference.

- When you get home, open the driver's side door and get out. The dog is still restrained by the rope closed in the passenger's door. Then go around to the right side and grab the rope with the knot in it *before* you open the door to release the dog. You are always in control.

When driving, keep the windows rolled up so the dog can't jump out.

Establish the Dog's Routine

As soon as you get your new dog home, take it to its bathroom area to relieve itself. Then put it in its Safe Space to settle down. Start to establish its routine immediately.

Here is an example of a good initial routine when you get your new

Take your new dog to its relief area regularly, and on leash.

trouble, you can consider leaving it unsupervised for a short time. Make it a short time: fifteen minutes to start. You'll soon see if the dog is going to wreck the place or if it has become accustomed to being loose in a house.

Avoid Damage

Each time any animal gets away with doing the wrong thing, it reinforces that bad behavior. Each time it misbehaves, it more likely to do it again. Avoid this. Avoid damage and avoid punishment. Don't give your dog the opportunity to learn to make mistakes. If you're not sure of what it will do, put it in its Space when you leave the room, even for five minutes. It's too late to punish if you come back and find a mess.

If You Must Be Away

Many dog owners have full-time jobs. If this meant they shouldn't own dogs, there would be even more homeless dogs in the world than there already are. Get a dog, but if you're not at home most of the day, make provisions for it to be comfortable and happy while you're at work.

If you're going to be gone eight or more hours at a time, don't get a puppy. Puppies need to be fed and to be taken out to eliminate far more often than do older dogs. If they aren't taken out, they will have to mess in their Safe Space, and you'll end up with a dog that gets used to sleeping in its mess and won't bother to wait. You'll also end up with a dog that barks a lot and

dog home: outside; feed; outside; socialize with family and other animals under close supervision; outside; back in the Safe Space for the night. Your routine will vary with your own schedule, but each new activity should be preceded by a trip outside to allow the dog to relieve itself. Soon, the dog will know why it's going outside. You will be surprised to find that your new dog will be housebroken almost automatically. Chapter 16 details the easy housebreaking process.

When the dog settles down to sleep during the socializing periods and shows no inclination to chew anything or to otherwise get into chews up anything within its reach because the pup will have nothing else to do while you're at work. Select one of the many adult dogs at shelters—they are literally dying for a home.

If you're at work all day, you might consider making the Safe Space for your dog larger than you would ordinarily. True, the dog might mess in part of it, but you can easily pick up the newspapers, and it's far better than forcing a dog to sleep in its own mess. You might even deliberately paper-train your dog, if it's small enough, by giving it a large Space covered with newspapers except for a separate box or bed to sleep in.

If you buy an adult dog, one or two meals and about four or five trips outside are adequate for a whole day, and you can still do this if you have a full-time job. If you buy a puppy, it needs three meals a day and about a dozen trips outside to train it.

If you get an adult dog, you can leave it a bowl or bucket of water, in case it gets thirsty. If you get a pup, it will upset the bucket, chew up the bowl, drink too much, and urinate all over its area.

If you get an older dog, you can leave its toys and its blanket in its Space while you're away. If you get a pup, you must pick up everything it can chew and swallow.

Don't plan to leave your dog tied outside on a chain while you are at work. Chaining a dog outside for long periods of time is not satisfac-tory because the dog is confined to a small area that soon becomes filthy and muddy, and a chained dog cannot escape bad weather, flies, or its enemies. Two or more dogs must never be tied outside where there is any chance that their chains could become entangled and strangle one or both of them.

Legal Considerations

Dog Licenses

Any dog turned in to a shelter by its owner becomes the legal prop-erty of the shelter. Any dog running loose and picked up by shelter per-sonnel or caught by a citizen and taken to a shelter must be held for redemption by its owner for a period of time that varies by locality but is not less than three days. If the dog is wearing a license, the owner may reclaim it after paying a fine. If the dog has no license, the owner must buy a license as well as paying a fine. If the owner has not claimed the dog after three days, it becomes the property of the shelter and can be sold or euthanized at the shelter's discretion.

Shelters can sell only those dogs that they legally own. When you buy a shelter dog, you will be required to buy a local dog license for it. Your receipt from the shelter and your name on the license certificate make you the dog's new legal owner, so put those papers away in a safe place. Occasionally former owners show up and demand the return of their dog, but they won't have a legal leg to stand on; the license tag and certificate you bought with the dog are written proof of your ownership.

Your Responsibilities

Strictly for legal purposes, the receipt you sign when you buy a dog from a shelter contains a disclaimer about the dog's future health and behavior. The minute you sign the papers and walk out the door with the dog, it's yours, and you are responsible for it and everything it does. When you buy a shelter dog, you cannot allow it to harm persons or property and try to assign responsibility to the shelter. If it bites a child as you are taking it to your car, you're responsible. If it gets away from you and is lost, it's up to you to find it; you signed the purchase agreement. If there is something wrong with the dog, you can't claim the shelter sold you defective merchandise, although many humane societies will contribute to veterinary care or will exchange the animal if it is found to be sick within a few days of purchase. Read your agreement carefully and be prepared for all eventualities.

Checklist for the Homecoming

1. Bring a well-fitting collar and leash, or buy one at shelters that sell them. Have a longer rope or leash at home to use when you walk your dog.
2. If you're getting a little puppy, bring a sturdy box or a carrier.
3. Have your Safe Space ready for your dog before you get it home.
4. Select your outside relief area before you need it, so you and the dog can get started right.
5. If possible, have on hand some of the food the dog has been eating. Change its diet gradually and be sure not to overfeed it, even if it's very thin. It's hard to housebreak a dog with diarrhea.
6. Keep all the papers you get with the dog, and put them in a safe place as soon as you get home. You'll need them to prove ownership and to show your veterinarian what medical treatment your dog has received at the shelter.
7. Be prepared to have infinite patience. Be prepared to be forgiving of mistakes. Be prepared to be surprised at how quickly the dog will learn your rules. Most of all, be prepared to find yourself wondering how you ever lived without that special dog.

Chapter Twelve
Sex—Who Needs It?

Dogs are very good at reproduction. They have too many puppies and they have them too often. About half of all animals put to death are adults, but the rest are puppies, innocently born into a world that has no room for them.

The average female dog can give birth to a litter of pups by the time she is a year old, and she can have another litter about every six months until her health fails. Female dogs don't have a menopause; they are able to reproduce until something goes terribly wrong with their bodies—something that can easily be fatal.

The tiny breeds of dogs may have only two or three pups in each litter, but the giant breeds often have ten or more. The number of pups that survive to weaning age averages about five per litter. It is easy to see that a female dog that is allowed to breed every time she is fertile will produce an average of ten living puppies every year, and within the next year, each of her female puppies will be old enough to produce ten puppies of its own! This abundant reproduction was of great value to the survival of the species when dogs were wild animals. Disease, predators, and starvation reduced their numbers and kept the population relatively low. Domestication has changed this situation. Now the surplus of dogs is so great that animal shelters kill them by the millions. Such a short, miserable life to be born to!

Although most of the population of the United States live in an urban or suburban setting, the old-time rural idea of allowing dogs to run loose persists. "Just open the door and let the dog out; it'll know how to come home." Maybe it will, but maybe it will be hit by a car, maybe it'll eat poison, be killed by a bigger

Mother (right), and son were found together.

83

Pregnant dogs are frequently abandoned at shelters, and shelters will try to find homes for all the pups.

dog, shot as a trespasser, lost, or stolen. For sure if it's a female, it will get pregnant every time it can. Remember, the cause of dog over-population is the owners who do not care enough for their animals to keep them safe from danger and death.

Preventing Unwanted Matings

Female dogs don't have to be spayed to keep them from having puppies, although spaying them is the easiest, the most certain, and the most convenient way to do it. To prevent unspayed female dogs from having puppies, the dogs just have to be prevented from mating. This means complete isolation from all fertile male dogs when they are capable of conceiving a litter. It means not allowing females to run loose. It means not chaining them in the yard where any passing dog can mate with them. It means not

ever allowing them to mate and produce puppies that nobody wants. No animal from a shelter should ever be allowed to produce more homeless dogs.

The Female Dog's Reproductive Cycle

Many female dogs get bred by accident because their owners don't recognize their fertile periods. This is particularly true of owners who have never had a female dog or who raised the dog from a puppy and don't realize what's happening to their pet.

Female dogs have reproductive activity occurring in cycles, usually twice a year. Veterinarians call these *estrus cycles;* laypersons refer to them as *heat periods.* It is only during the fertile part of these cycles that a female can become pregnant.

The normal estrus cycle or heat period of the dog is divided into four distinct phases. Veterinarians call the first phase *proestrus;* laypersons say that the dog is "coming in heat." Proestrus lasts from 4 to 13 days, averages 9 days in length, and starts at the first appearance of bleeding from the vulva. During this time, the female usually will not permit a male to mate with her. Her ova are not yet ready and she cannot get pregnant at this time.

The next several days in a female's cycle is called *estrus,* or "in heat," because the female will stand and move her tail to the side, allowing the male to mate with her. During this period, the vulva is swollen and soft and the vulvar discharge is yellowish, not red like blood. Inexperienced owners have a tendency to think that once the bleeding stops, their female dog is out of heat. This is the exact opposite of the truth! It is *only* during this time that a female dog can get pregnant.

The period after estrus in the cycle is *metestrus.* During this period, the size of the vulva gradually returns to normal. Within about nine days, the female dog is "out of heat." Dog breeders summarize the female's cycle this way: nine days going into heat, nine days in heat, nine days going out of heat. These figures are approximate. Normal individuals may have phases of the cycle half as long or twice as long.

If the normal female dog is bred during her estrus period, she will become pregnant. Her abdomen will enlarge, her mammary glands will develop, and her body will get ready to whelp and care for a litter of pups. About 63 days after breeding, the pregnant female will seek a secluded place to deliver her litter. The birth process in dogs and dog-like animals is called *whelping.*

False Pregnancy

Even if she was not bred, the body of a normal, healthy female continues to produce the hormones of pregnancy during the 9 weeks following her heat period. At the time she would have had puppies had she been mated, the healthy

Summary of the Female Dog's Cycle

- The young female dog will come into heat for the first time on an average at 7 to 12 months of age.
- The first signs will be a bloody discharge and an enlargement of her vulva. This will last about nine days. Dog breeders call this period "coming into heat."
- After about nine days, this period ends. The discharge will become more yellow, and the female will accept and mate with the male. She is then "in heat."
- During the next two months, her hormones get her ready for motherhood. If she had a fertile mating, her abdomen will enlarge as the puppies develop. She will whelp approximately 63 days after she was mated.
- If no fertile mating took place, the female dog will undergo a false pregnancy, which may be very dramatic, may be almost unnoticeable to the owner, or anything in between.
- After that period, she'll either be raising her litter or in anestrus until it's time for her cycles to start again.

non-pregnant female will undergo a false pregnancy, or *pseudocyesis,* "pseudo" meaning false and "cyesis" meaning pregnancy. This condition occurs in all female dogs with normal reproductive organs, but it is not always noticeable to their owners. Many of their pets don't look or act strange during their false pregnancy, but some will behave as though they were actually going to have a litter. They will develop enlarged mammary glands and may even have milk in the glands. They might seek out a secluded place and make a nest for the puppies they believe they're going to have. They may pant and shake like a female dog in labor. They may take a toy and "mother" it; refusing to let anyone take it away from them.

Pseudocyesis will last from a few days to two weeks. Then the dog enters the *anestrus* phase of her reproductive cycle. This means "without estrus." She'll stay in anestrus for three or four months, then start her reproductive cycle all over again.

During anestrus, an unspayed female that is not raising puppies will act just like one that has been spayed, but for about one month in every six, she will be undergoing activity of her reproductive cycle. People with female pets would rather not have this occur for a variety of reasons.

1. There's always the chance that the female will accidentally get loose or otherwise contact a male dog and get pregnant.
2. She will have a discharge that stains the rugs, car seats, and furniture, and she will attract male dogs to your yard and otherwise make a nuisance of herself.

3. If she is a female that undergoes a full false pregnancy, she'll act very strange for a while, and not at all like the pet she's supposed to be.
4. Most important, she'll be in danger of some of the life-threatening effects of her hormones.

Female Reproductive Diseases

Mammary Cancer

At least 25 percent of all female dogs that are not spayed sooner or later will develop mammary tumors, which are the same as breast cancer in humans. Unspayed female dogs develop this condition most often when they are middle-aged, from five to ten years old. As with human breast cancer, dogs' mammary tumors can kill them, and as with humans, dogs can be treated with surgery, radiation, and chemotherapy. The treatment is expensive, debilitating, and often unsuccessful; however, unlike humans, dogs can be almost completely prevented from developing this cancer.

In medicine, human or veterinary, the term *never* is not used. Doctors say *seldom,* or *rarely.* However, in the case of the female dog spayed before her ovaries have matured, there are so few known cases of mammary cancer that *never* becomes an appropriate term. If your female puppy is spayed before her first heat period, you can forget about her developing this malignancy.

With females that are spayed after they have had only a few heat periods, the surgery that removes the ovarian hormones lessens their chances of developing this cancer. But by the time a female is four or five years old, she has had eight or ten heat periods, and the hormonal damage is done. Therefore, spaying her after she is three or four years old will have little effect on tumor development. Obviously, it is to a female dog's great advantage to be spayed before she is six months old. It keeps her from developing mammary gland cancer, a killer disease.

Pyometra

Pyometra is a medical term that means "pus in the uterus." This condition is sometimes called an infected uterus, because the uterus is full of pus that resembles a bacterial infection. Pyometra in dogs is primarily caused by repeated hormone stimulation of the uterine lining, and is common in older dogs that have had many heat periods. Obviously, spayed female dogs never develop this condition because their uterus has been surgically removed.

Pyometra can be more immediately fatal than mammary cancer. The victims of this condition often die from septicemia unless treated promptly and vigorously with surgery and drugs.

Other Female Reproductive Diseases

Less common than mammary cancer and pyometra, female dogs can also develop ovarian or uterine cancer. A spayed dog has neither ovaries nor a uterus, nor the hormones that promote mammary tumors. All of these deadly conditions can be prevented by spaying.

Importance of Spaying

"Shouldn't my dog have a heat period before she's spayed? Shouldn't she have a litter first?" Veterinarians are often asked these questions. The answer is obvious. The female dog should have a heat period *only* if the owner wants to increase the dog's chances of a life-threatening disease, or if the owner wants to add to the immense problem of pet overpopulation. The concerned pet owner knows the correct answer—*spay!*

The growing trend is for humane societies to require sterilization of all dogs and puppies adopted from their shelters. Many societies include at least part of the cost of the surgery in the purchase price of the animal. These societies sometimes have the older dogs spayed before they are released for adoption, but not the puppies because six months has been the traditional age at which to spay, and most puppies are adopted before they are six months old. Modern methods of veterinary anesthesia and surgery have changed this idea. Now puppies often are surgically

Even the cutest puppies can fail to find a home.

sterilized at as young as eight weeks of age. Research has shown that this procedure is entirely safe, and that the younger the animal, the shorter the recovery period and the fewer the side effects. Surgeons have found that operating on very young animals is quicker and easier. With early-age spaying and neutering, puppies are already sterilized when they are adopted. This eliminates the problem of owners who agree to have their pets sterilized, but who neglect to have it done.

It is less expensive to have your dog spayed when she's young and healthy than to try to save her life when she's old and sick. Even if the shelter from which you get your dog doesn't subsidize the surgery, have your dog spayed and pay for it yourself. If you consider the cost of comparable human surgery including hospitalization, anesthesiologist, surgeon, laboratory fees—your vet-

erinarian is very inexpensive. Your dog must have the same care as a human patient: It must have lab tests to be sure it is ready for surgery; it must be hospitalized for at least one day; it must be given a pre-anesthetic drug to make it drowsy and then an anesthetic to put it to sleep for the duration of the operation; it must be watched carefully during the surgery to be sure the anesthetic level is correct; it must be operated on by a skilled surgeon who has had years of training and who uses the same sterile technique and equipment as does a human surgeon; it must be supervised until it is entirely out of the anesthetic, and if needed, it must be given the same drugs and antibiotics as are used for humans; it must have the same follow-up care and suture removal as a human patient. In spite of the similarity of the procedure, routine spay and neuter surgery on a dog is less than a tenth as expensive as the exact same surgery performed on a human.

If you let your female dog get old and fat, the surgeon has the same problem as does a human surgeon who must do abdominal surgery on an old fat lady. It's much more difficult and much more time consuming, therefore much more expensive and dangerous. And if your dog is not only old and fat, but is also critically ill with pyometra, mammary cancer, or both, the surgery will take a great deal of time, skill, drugs, and equipment. Your old fat dog will be a poor surgical risk and much more postsurgical care, hospitalization, and medication will be required if your dog is to survive. Even though the total cost will be less than a tenth of what a human hospital would charge for the same services, Blue Cross doesn't pay it; you'll have to pay it yourself or lose your old friend. You might pay it and still lose your old friend if she's sick enough, so protect both your dog and your wallet—have your pup spayed while she is very young.

Neutering the Male Dog

Humane societies almost without exception insist that the male dogs they offer for adoption be neutered. *Neutered, altered,* and *fixed* are all terms for castration, the surgical removal of the testicles. Neutering of all male pet dogs is an excellent idea, but not for the reasons usually stated by the societies.

Humane societies exist to help animals. Their job is endless because of the vast number of dogs and puppies for which there are no homes. One of the main goals is to prevent the birth of unwanted animals, so humane societies promote surgical sterilization as a method of population control. But neutering your dog won't help reduce the number of puppies that are born. Why not? No owner who loves his dog lets it run loose, female or male, neutered or not. If your dog doesn't run loose, it will never sire a litter accidentally, because it will never accidentally come into contact with an unspayed female dog.

It is only female dogs running loose that have unplanned pregrancies. Any male dog running loose will mate with every female in heat that it encounters. Since every fertile male dog can sire dozens of litters a year, if your dog is neutered and can't be a sire, someone else's dog will sire that litter in its place. A fertile female running at large won't go unmated because your dog is castrated. With that in mind, population control is not the big reason that all pet male dogs should be neutered.

Male Dogs' Reproductive Diseases

As with females, males have health problems that are associated with their reproductive organs, but these problems are not as common and usually not as severe as the problems of females. Testicular cancer does occur, and it can kill its victims. Prostate cancer is rare in dogs, but prostatic hyperplasia is not, and while this condition isn't a killer, it can make a male dog very sick. *Perianal adenomas,* skin tumors around the anal area, are common only in male dogs and can be a very serious medical problem. These conditions can be prevented and even cured by neutering.

The Influence of Neutering on Behavior

As important as neutering is to the health of the male dog, it is far more important to the behavior of the dog. This is a subject often overlooked: an unneutered male dog is going to act like a male, and training won't completely overcome it. Male dogs don't go into heat like females. They can be sexually active all the time. While obnoxious sexual activity like mounting and trying to mate with sofa cushions or the legs of children is fairly easily overcome by simple and consistent discipline, some sexual activities of male dogs are not.

"He won't roam if he's neutered. He won't fight if he's neutered. He won't disobey if he's neutered." These reasons are used to encourage owners to have the surgery performed. It would be wonderful if these reasons were true. Unfortunately, they are not.

By nature, a dog is an intelligent animal. In the wild, dogs live by hunting. Sex in a dog's life is something that takes place only occasionally when the opportunity permits, but exploring and hunting are a healthy dog's constant activities. A dog doesn't roam only to look for females; it roams because it is its nature to be a curious and active hunter. A few dogs will be porch potatoes and never leave the yard, but most, neutered or not, will explore for miles if they are allowed to run loose. If you think all you have to do to keep your dog in your own yard is to have it neutered, save your money and your veterinarian's time. You'll be disappointed when it doesn't work that way.

Fighting with other dogs is an inborn behavior, not only of males but of females. It occurs in neutered and unneutered animals alike, and it's usually caused by dog's territorial instincts, not by the sex drive. The case of male dogs fighting over a female in heat is the only example of fighting that could be considered to be related only to sex. All other examples of inter-dog aggression are caused by something else. Neutering your male dog might reduce its fighting tendencies, but neutering alone won't eliminate them.

Will a neutered dog be easier to obedience train? Don't count on it. If you habitually train your dog in the presence of females in heat, you might notice that a neutered dog will do less sniffing around the female dogs; otherwise you won't notice a thing. Will he be less aggressive toward people? Nope. Sex is not why a dog bites a person; dominance is.

Scent Marking

Unneutered male dogs mark their territory with the scent of their urine. This is a highly unpleasant feature of a male dog's normal behavior that is positively influenced by neutering. If it's a house dog and if the owners care anything at all about their household furnishings, neutering is essential.

All male dogs that aren't surgically altered will scent mark. They mark their territory, or what they perceive as their territory, with small amounts of their urine. They will mark their territory in many, many places. They will do it over and over again to keep the scent fresh. Wolves do it, foxes do it, cats and lions do it—but dogs do it in your house. They are telling the world: "Here's my scent; this is my place."

Not all dogs scent mark to the same extent. Dogs in multiple-dog households mark more because they feel that they are in competition with the others. Cats, birds, even a new baby or a new girlfriend or boyfriend are perceived as competition by a dog and stimulate it to scent mark. A move to another house will cause scent marking of the new area even though it contains all of the already marked old furniture.

An unneutered male dog, well housebroken, in a home with no other pets, might not scent mark very often. It might not lift its leg against the couch until it sees another dog through the window, and it might not do it on visitors' pants legs unless the visitors are dog-owners themselves and smell like a strange dog. Sooner or later, no matter how well trained or how submissive it may be, the unneutered male dog will squirt urine somewhere in your house. No dog scent marks because it needs to urinate, and no amount of punishment will entirely abolish the behavior. The unneutered dog really can't help itself; it's a hormone-related act. The male dog feels compelled to leave its own personal scent in its area, therefore, if you decide to keep an unneutered male dog for a house pet, get brown carpeting and yellow drapes, and don't get a nice white bedspread.

Almost no dog neutered before puberty will scent mark. Puberty in most dogs is around six months of age, but to be safe, have your pup operated on at four months. If you get an older dog, try to have the surgery done before you even bring it home to eliminate the hormonal cause for the behavior. At least, have the dog neutered before you allow it to roam unsupervised in your house.

Many dogs are neutered only after the household is yellow and smelly and the owner is disgusted. Even after a dog is several years old, castration will diminish scent marking, but it often takes months until the change is apparent. Whatever the age of the dog, neutering is certainly worth having done! It will make a difference eventually, if not immediately.

Watchdogs

The dog that is spayed or castrated will be a better watchdog than the dog that is not. Dogs bark and threaten intruders because the canine species has an inborn instinct, called territorial aggression, to protect its home. This instinct is related to hunting food, not to reproduction. Some dogs are glad to see anybody and never ever bark when the doorbell rings, but the average adult dog sounds the alarm, loudly, at every strange noise. A spayed female won't be out of action because of reproductive function at the time she's supposed to be a guard. A neutered male won't be influenced by an intruder who recently handled a female dog. Dogs' aggressive tendencies are affected very little by surgical removal of their reproductive organs.

In summary, keep this in mind: Your dog doesn't need sex for a "full life." Don't assume that your dogs have human feelings. Don't ever think your dogs "need" sex. Remember, dogs don't think like people. They don't feel "less of a dog" if they are not sexually active. In the case of a female, your spayed dog will live a far longer, healthier, and less troublesome life than if you had denied her the benefits of surgery. Your neutered male dog won't miss sex, either. Nor will your couch and drapes miss the smelly yellow stains!

Chapter Thirteen

Submission Training— You're the Boss

Every dog trainer has a different opinion about kindness, discipline and punishment. Some trainers say, "No force! Never punish!" Some say, "You gotta make them obey you!" Both trainers are right, and both are wrong.

Dogs are not much different from small children. Dogs and children instinctively try to get their own way. They seek to avoid restraint, resist sharing their food or toys, and don't want to go to bed (or to their Safe Space) at bedtime. But dogs don't hit and cry and stamp their feet. They don't steal hubcaps or run up big bills on your credit card. Dogs bite.

The Biting Dog

Dogs that bite their owners often end up at animal shelters because owners quickly become disenchanted with untrustworthy animals, and their cute puppy isn't so cute anymore. They've given it lots of love and attention, and the ungrateful brute doesn't hesitate to take a chunk out of them, often seemingly unprovoked. The children are afraid to walk near its food dish, to touch its toys, or even to pet it. Instead of being a playmate and companion, the dog is a menace, a tyrant in the household.

When you selected your shelter dog, you made every effort to avoid a dominant-aggressive type. You certainly were able to avoid any dog that is actually aggressive and any dog that is a hysterical fear-biter, since those are obvious behaviors. However, you might have unknowingly purchased a dog that is usually good-tempered but that might growl or bite in certain circumstances; it is not vicious; it simply has not been taught that it must regard you and your family as its boss at all times. If you've bought a dog like this, don't give up. You can overcome its lack of early training and make it safe and pleasant for you and your family to handle.

Who's the Boss?

There are children who are perfect little angels no matter how hard their parents try to spoil them, and there are dogs that would never bite anyone. The process of domestication has selected dogs of a basically submissive nature toward humans; most of them will never challenge people for boss status. These dogs will never become aggressive biters no matter how they are treated; however, most dogs and children will be as bossy as their "parents" will allow. Owners and parents must teach their dogs and children the rules of society, but since dogs and children do not have the same mental abilities, we cannot teach them the rules in the same way.

Very few puppies are genetically predisposed toward what psychol-

ogists call "alpha" behavior, the desire to always be the boss in their social groups. These puppies will growl if anyone comes near their food or toys; they will grab at hands and snarl aggressively in play; they will resist any sort of restraint such as being picked up or leashed by snarling and trying to bite. Genetically dominant puppies are more likely to be males, but breed and sex are only a part of a dog's tendency toward dominance.

The average puppy of either sex will try to get its own way, but will quickly and easily submit to mild, appropriate discipline. Only those young dogs that never receive mild discipline learn that when they growl or snap at their humans, they win every time. These dogs are not genetically dominant types. They learn dominance just as an undisciplined child learns to be a brat.

If a dog is allowed to become the boss, it will bite whenever it is challenged and it will bite any challenger. The generous and unsuspecting owner often makes it easy for the puppy to become the boss. "Keep away from the dog while it's eating!" "Don't pick it up—it doesn't like that!" "Let it have that toy." The young dog gets its own way constantly as the human members of its pack avoid getting bitten by relinquishing control. Soon the dog has established itself as the alpha animal. It growls if a person approaches its bowl or its bed. It initiates rough and aggressive play, and jumps up on everyone with impunity. If it is challenged in any way, it has ro inhibitions against biting.

What is the result of the dog becoming the boss? A surprising number of owners love their dog enough to put up with a dog that will bite, but they can't consider it to be a very good pet. Even more owners dispose of the biter because they or their children are afraid of it. They worry that it will bite someone, often leading to a lawsuit. Some people lose their tempers and beat the stuffings out of the dog to "teach it a lesson." None of these are good solutions for the humans or for the cog.

Take a look at the way dogs establish dominance over one another. If a pup does something that its mother doesn't like, she pushes it away, growls, or actually grabs it by the neck and holds it down, snarling. Very seldom does a mother dog actually hurt one of her own puppies, but from the shrill cries of the offending pup, you'd think it was being killed. The puppy soon learns the lesson that Mother is the boss, at least until weaning.

An adult dog establishes dominance over another dog in exactly the same way. It growls, threatens to bite, or actually does bite the offender. When the boss dog has established its position, it rarely has to do more than growl to make the other dog give in. But if a weaker or younger dog doesn't respond to the growl, the boss will grab it by the throat and, snarling fiercely, pin it to the ground. The offender seldom fights back. It cowers or rolls over on its back, and it assumes a submissive posture.

The relationship a dog has with its boss pack leader is the one we want our dogs to have with us: to not challenge us for boss status. We never want our own dogs to offer to bite us. We want our dogs to respond if we "growl." We don't want our dogs to fear us, but to respect our authority. We want to establish this relationship qu ckly and easily without using any cruelty or causing any pain.

Submission Testing and Training

Submission training consists of only one thing: teaching your puppy or dog to allow you, without any resistance, to place it in a submissive position and to hold it there for as long as you like.

Submission training is not a mystical method of influencing a dog's attitude toward you. It is a method of using dogs' natural behavior to your advantage, and using it in a way that dogs instinctively understand. You cause the dog to assume a submissive physical posture in relation to yourself. By doing so, you cause it to assume a submissive attitude toward you. The results of submission training are immediate and long-lasting. This sounds too simple to work, but it does.

The dog that is trained to be submissive toward its owners will not be timid or cowardly. It will not be afraid of people, but you can be confident that it will not bite you. The submissive dog will be respectful and will not resist any kind of non-painful handling including grooming its belly or touching its food.

Submission training is not punishment—it is training!

All dogs need a submission test, which is nothing more than your first attempt at placing the dog in a submissive position. You might have already done this when you examined dogs and puppies at the shelter (see pages 50–51). If the dog shows no resistance when you place it in the submissive position, it gets a perfect score. If it resists for only a few seconds, it gets an almost-perfect score. If it shows more resis-

Submission training will help these dogs respond to discipline.

tance, it lets you know that it needs more submission training.

Every dog that spends its lifetime in the company of humans—and that means every one of our dogs—should be submissive to us. Since the vast majority of puppies and most adult dogs are born submissive to humans, the whole process of submission training will take a total of ten minutes. It will be nothing more than a test to see if the dog is submissive. The importance of this test is that it will detect those pups and dogs that will *not* be naturally submissive to people, and will allow their owners the chance to alter the dog's behavior before any damage is done.

Submission training produces a powerful inhibition against a puppy or dog ever biting its owner. If every puppy had a submission test, and if every puppy had a few minutes of submission training, no owner would ever be bitten by his or her own dog.

When to Do the Submission Test

Do the test the day you get your puppy. It only takes a few minutes, and most puppies will regard it as play. When the test is followed up by three or four sessions of submission training, your puppy will become submissive to your handling. Then you can forget about the training; ordinarily your puppy will be submissive toward you for life. If it ever shows by its actions that it would like to challenge your authority, you

can repeat the minute's worth of training a few more times.

If you get an adult dog, start the testing and training as soon as the two of you are comfortable with each other, which is usually after you have lived together for a day or two. As soon as you are sufficiently comfortable to brush and comb your new dog, you should perform the submission test. Just as with puppies, most adult dogs will regard this training as play.

Is Submission Training Cruel?

Of course not! Only this training assures that your dog will never bite you. Should all dogs have a submission test? Should all dogs have this training? Yes, even the few that are naturally very timid and obviously submissive. The test and training will help them learn that handling by their owners won't hurt them. There's only one way to find out if your dog is naturally submissive to you. Try the test. If your dog is submissive, forget it; you will have lost nothing and you will have gained confidence in your dog's good nature.

Remember, dogs don't speak your language, even though you can teach them to respond to certain words and phrases like "Sit" or "Wanna go out?" Dogs also learn what some of your unspoken actions mean, such as when you open the refrigerator door or put on your coat, but dogs never understand spoken explanations. You can shout, "I'm going to kill you if you do that again," and all your dog hears is your harsh voice. It might realize by your tone that you're angry, but it has no way of knowing why.

Dog books tell you to stand tall, to look the dog in the eye, to speak in an authoritarian tone of voice. In other words, to act "alpha" toward your dog. But since you're not a dog, you can stand as tall as you like, stare into its eyes all day long, and shout at the top of your lungs, and your dog may not relate your actions to the alpha status. In fact, your dog might not notice your posture or your stare because a human's two-legged stance is vastly different from a dog on four legs.

Don't think there's something the matter with you if your dog doesn't respond in the way the books describe. Those instructions don't always work because it takes a little more positive action than good posture and a steady gaze to show your dog that you really are the boss.

There is *no* cruelty, pain, or mistreatment involved in teaching your dog to be submissive to you, even though some dogs might seem to think so at first. Human sociologists call this sort of training, "tough love," because, when necessary, you do it for the dogs' own good. Certainly it is more cruel to allow a dog to become or to remain a dominant and aggressive biter than to train it to be submissive through tough love. Dogs that bite are no pleasure to own and often are euthanized because of their behavior. Do you want to keep a dog you are afraid will bite you? Of course not, and neither does anyone else.

Physical Abuse

Never, never, hit, beat, whip, or strike a dog with your hand or any other object. Not only is beating a dog inhumane, it is ineffective as a method of discipline. Hitting and beating don't produce the results you want. A dog does not understand that a beating is punishment for past bad behavior. All the dog senses is that its human is causing it extreme fear and pain. The dog can respond to fear and pain in one of two ways: by running away from you or by fighting back and trying to bite you. Neither response is desirable. You want your dog to love and respect you, not to fear you and never to bite you. When you give your dog submission training, you will attain this goal.

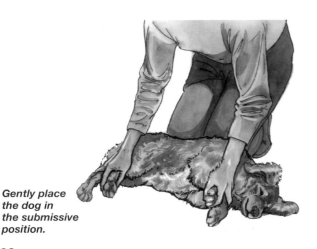

Gently place the dog in the submissive position.

The Submissive Position

A dog in the submissive position is lying on its side with all four feet held by its owner. It remains lying on its side without the slightest struggle for as long as its owner holds it there. Believe it or not, that's all there is to it.

It is not necessary or desirable for the dog to be taught to stay in that position without being held. The minute the owner lets go of its feet, the dog is free to get up.

To place the dog in the submissive position, kneel down and gently pull the dog over onto its side with its back toward your knees. This is easier if you can get the dog to lie down in the usual way and then pull it onto its side. Never grab the dog's legs and slam it down onto the ground. Never be rough.

Hold both of the dog's front legs with your left hand and both back legs with your right. Press your forearms gently on the dog's body to keep it down. Hold the dog in this position for a count of five after the dog stops all struggling, then release it and give it a little mild praise.

This training might seem like magic because, once the dog accepts the position without a struggle, the resulting behavior modification is profound and durable. The dog learns that you are able to restrain it, that you are physically dominant to it, that you are the boss and you are never to be challenged. It learns this very quickly, without any cruelty whatever: no beating, no shouting, no yanking on a choke collar.

While you are holding your dog in the submissive position, don't say anything to it unless it struggles. If it shows great resistance to the position, you should reprimand it. Speak a little harshly if it squirms; speak sharply if it struggles violently or tries to bite. Never speak soothingly to the dog while it is struggling. A dog associates soothing talk with praise and approval; struggling is *not* approved behavior; therefore, you don't praise it for struggling. Struggling is bad behavior; if it struggles, you verbally correct it while continuing to restrain it. Holding the dog in the submissive position is not punishment—it is a demonstration to it that you are the boss.

Many puppies and dogs will hardly resist at all the first time they are placed in the submissive position, even less the second time, and none at all by the third time. They will lie there and wait to get their tummies scratched. Those that struggle a little stop as soon as they discover that they are not being hurt but that they can't get away. These dogs can, for all practical purposes, be considered to be graduates of the submissive-training program. You should do the exercise two or three more times just to assure yourself that your dog will never bite you.

A few dogs and even puppies will put up a terrific fight when they are forced into the submissive position. It is the fighters who benefit most from this submission training, since it is the fighters who aren't submissive and will become aggressive biters unless they receive training to prevent it.

This is a very important reminder: The use of the submissive position is a training technique only! It is *never* used as a punishment for anything a dog does except acts of aggression toward the owner.

Enforcement of the Submissive Position

Never let go of a dog until it submits and lies still without any struggle whatever. A really dominant dog will do terrible things while being held in the submissive position. Besides thrashing violently, it may snap at anything near its mouth, growl or cry loudly, even urinate and defecate all over the place. What should you do under these circumstances? Nothing. Simply keep on holding the dog down until the dog gives up in exhaustion and accepts your dominance by lying still for a count of five. Hold it there if it takes all day. Then release it, praise it mildly, and clean up the mess.

Psychologists call the procedure of enforcement until an animal stops struggling, *flooding* or *extinguishing*, because the dog's nervous system is flooded with the stimulus (holding it in the submissive position) until the undesirable behavior (resisting) is extinguished.

"Oh, I could never do that to a dog! I could never be that cruel!"

This owner is willing to allow his dog to be aggressive toward himself and other people. This owner suffers the consequences when his dog bites him. His dog also suffers the consequences because, after it has bitten him badly enough, he gets rid of it. Since nobody wants a biter, the dog dies.

Submission Training for Fear-Biters: Many puppies and dogs resist being placed in the submissive position, not out of aggression, but out of fear. This doesn't change the training method at all. Submission training will actually reform a fear-biter, at least as far as its owner is concerned. The training will teach it not to bite even if it is frightened. It teaches it that no harm will come to it from the owner's handling, that it cannot successfully resist by biting, and that it cannot escape by biting. Fearful dogs usually learn to lie still much quicker than aggressive ones, but a confirmed fear-biter may struggle as violently as a dominant dog at first. For the owner's safety, some dogs may need to be muzzled when the training is begun.

Gentle Submission Training: The dog that automatically crouches, rolls over onto its back or side or perhaps urinates when you approach is already submissive. It needs very gentle submission training. You should be very gentle when you place it in the submissive position. Make it fun and play. Never hold these dogs in the submissive position if they have assumed the position by themselves.

When you place these timid dogs in the position, you are teaching them that they have nothing to fear from you. You are teaching them that, while you are the boss, you are a benevolent boss and won't hurt them. Paradoxically, this training will help the dog that urinates on your shoes become more confident and outgrow this behavior. Then you'll have to teach it not to jump up on you.

If you have a terribly fearful little puppy and you want to be sure that it won't become a fear-biter, start submission training by merely lifting it with both your hands under its stomach so its feet don't touch the ground. Hold it there for the five seconds. When it no longer resists being lifted, hold it in your arms on its back like a baby. When it doesn't resist, place it gently on its side in the submissive position on the ground.

Repeat Submission Training If Needed

A few dogs will need continued submission training over weeks or even months. These are the ones that persist in struggling when placed in the submissive position or continue to growl or snap at their owners when they are handled. Be careful not to mistake play growling for the real thing. If a dog gets too excited and growls in play, you are playing too rough with it. Simply stop playing and let the dog calm down.

Some dogs seem to accept the submissive position without a struggle, but will still growl at their owners around their food or toys. For these dogs, the submission exercise should be performed two or three times in each training session for as long as the dog growls at the owner. Place the dog in the submissive position, hold it there for a count of five, then allow it to get up and be praised. Work on "sit" for a minute or two, and then repeat the submission exercise.

Muzzles for Known Biters

Almost all dogs, no matter how dominant and aggressive they have learned to be, can be trained to relinquish their boss status by submission training. In some cases the training can be a formidable task. A known biter should be muzzled before it is placed in the submissive position. It might have to be muzzled and forced to submit dozens of times before it will be safe to train without a muzzle. In such cases, the muzzle should be one constructed of a cone of nylon or leather that fits snugly over the dog's face. The dog should never have its mouth tied tightly with a rope or a leash; that in itself is painful and causes additional resentment. A wire basket muzzle should not be used as the dog may thrash around and hit the handler with the muzzle.

Even known biters that are very dominant-aggressive can be changed by submission training. The more violently the dog resists, the more it needs this training and the more frequently the exercises should be repeated. For a really aggressive dog, twice a day will produce the fastest, most lasting results. Once the aggressive dog automatically gives up and lies still when placed in the submissive position, the dog may be placed on a maintenance schedule of submission training a few times a week. A dog that has learned to be dominant-aggressive may cooperate only after many weeks of difficult and tiring sessions. With really determined dogs, it takes a really determined owner to stick to it. Is it worth it? That depends on how much you care about your dog—and your anatomy. Are you willing to have the dog put to death because nobody will live with it? Are you willing to be bitten by your own dog? Or are you willing to expend the effort to teach it that you, its owner, are the boss in all circumstances?

Include the Family in the Training

Once the dog or puppy is submissive to its primary owner and can be placed and held in the submissive position without any resentment, it should be willing to submit to being placed in position by anyone in the household. If a member of the family is reluctant or too young to restrain the dog, the primary owner can restrain it while the other member strokes its head, back, and legs. This helps to convince the dog that it is physically submissive to every family member, including children.

Continued Training

After sufficient training, any now-submissive dog should respond to only a word ("NO!") if it makes the slightest attempt to resist handling by its owner. If the dog ever starts to growl or bite its owner, the owner should *instantly* place it in the submissive position and hold it there while the owner "growls." The position is used as punishment *only* for acts of aggression by the dog toward its owner. It reinforces the idea in the dog's mind that it must never bite the hand that feeds it. Under no circumstances should the owner back off and let the dog get away with even one tiny growl.

Better Watchdogs

Your dog will be a better watchdog if it has submission training. If you're afraid your dog will be so submissive that it won't be a watchdog, don't worry. Submission training teaches the dog to submit to you and your family, not to strangers on your property. Even the most ferocious watchdog should never bite its owners. A dog's instinct to guard its territory is very strong and is not directly related to the instinct to try to be the boss animal. Submission training will insure that your watchdog will take orders from you and will not bite people you don't want bitten. It will make it possible for you to call your dog off guard and safely admit your guests.

The Right to Bite?

Should a dog ever bite a person? The best answer would be *never*. The most realistic answer would be almost never. It is common knowl-

edge that many dogs will instinctively attack a stranger who enters its home territory, and many dogs are kept primarily for that reason. There is no question that a large dog presents a formidable threat to trespassers. A dog that attacks someone molesting its owner is considered to be a valiant protector. A dog with a mouthful of snarling teeth is a better deterrent to car thieves than any mechanical alarm. The problem is, a dog has no way of judging if a trespasser is a thief or the mail carrier. It has no way of telling an attack from a friendly hug. Your lawyer will tell you to be very careful before you ever permit your dog to bite.

How to Punish a Dog

A dog should receive punishment only if the punishment will be effective to eliminate unwanted behavior. In many cases, punishing a dog at all is not effective, unwarranted, and cruel. A dog must never be punished in a way that it cannot understand or at a time even one second remote from the bad behavior.

Psychologists call punishment, *adversive conditioning,* or *negative conditioning* because it is intended to eliminate an action by making the action unpleasant for the perpetrator. Negative conditioning occurs at several levels:

1. Withholding praise or approval is the most mild form of punishment.

2. Verbal reprimands (scolding or yelling) are effective as a warning for sensitive dogs, but are ineffective in eliminating unwanted behavior in less sensitive animals.

3. Shaking the scruff of the neck is the way a mother dog punishes her pups. A dog will understand a shaking only if it is done at the instant of the infraction.

4. In obedience training, punishment is most often administered by a jerk on the choke chain. This usually mild adverse stimulus is used both for training ("Heel," when the dog is not in the correct position), and for correction ("Sit," when the dog gets up without permission). A dog disobeys a command only because it has received insufficient training to teach it to obey, so the disobedient dog should have more training, not punishment. Commands must be reinforced. Again, and again, and again. If a dog is properly trained, if the stimulus to obey is stronger than the stimulus to disobey, it will do what it's been trained to do.

5. Punishment for such infractions as chewing shoes or messing in the house is completely inappropriate. This sort of bad behavior should be treated by prevention: Shoes should be picked up and dogs should be taught where to eliminate.

Chapter Fourteen

Dogs, Children, the Elderly, and the Disabled

This little girl has a lap full of puppies.

Don't buy a dog just for the children. Buy a dog only if you want one for yourself, because a dog will be entirely your responsibility if your children are young. Your time and your effort will be required to care for it, to train it, and to supervise whenever your children interact with it. Never, never buy a dog for your children with the attitude that, if it doesn't work out, you can take it back to the shelter. Children become immensely attached to their pets. If you decide later that the dog was not a good idea and you don't keep it, it's entirely possible that your children will grieve just as though they've lost a member of the family. Worse, they will feel that it's your fault—you took something very precious away from them. They could have their faith in you seriously disrupted. If you took away their dog, what else might you take away? If you lie and tell them the dog died or ran away, how could they feel that anything in life was permanent or safe? Is it worth it? When you have children and you get a dog, you should plan to have the dog for keeps.

Pets, especially dogs, can provide a wonderful experience for a child. Dogs can teach a child about responsibility, kindness, consideration, and companionship. Dogs can also teach a child about fear, cruelty, and neglect. So, before you buy a dog for your children, be sure they'll get the right message.

What Kind of Dog Is Best for Children?

What kind of dog should you get if you have children? There are only two important considerations: First, you, the parent, must like and admire the type of dog you choose. Don't pick one you don't like just because someone tells you it's "good with children." If you like big dogs, don't get a tiny one; if you hate big ones, go ahead and get a toy breed. If you get a dog you don't like, everything it does wrong will be magnified in your mind, and you'll always think another choice would have been better.

Second, any dog you buy for children must, of course, not be a biter. This doesn't mean that you must find a dog that is already used to children. "Not a biter" means only that the dog must not be excessively fearful nor excessively dominant by nature. It must not have learned to fear children nor learned to dominate children. Any other behavior problems the dog might have are incidental; you can, with training, alter them. If it says on the dog's shelter card, "not good with small children," take their word for it and don't buy that dog.

A child and a puppy will learn from each other.

Consider the Age of the Child

What can a parent expect from a child in the way of interest in a dog and ability to care for it? This depends, of course, on the age and level of maturity of the child. A child in the pre-walking stage will enjoy looking at a dog and "talking" to it, will touch it and crawl toward it out of curiosity, but will have no more understanding of a dog's feelings than it would of the feelings of another infant.

The child of one-to-two years old walks well and will approach a dog expecting to play with it. This child must be taught not to cause pain by grabbing or poking the dog. Remember, a dog that learns to fear a child will bite one in self-defense.

Children who are older than two or three love to play with a gentle dog. At this age, a child and a dog can become very close; the child may actually prefer the company of the dog to the company of people. Four-year-old children can learn to pour out dog food and to take the water bowl to the sink for an adult to fill. They can assist in grooming the dog and walking it on a leash, if the dog is trained not to pull them down.

Up to about ten years old, children can help care for a dog, but only under adult supervision. As children mature, they can assume more responsibility, such as feeding the dog on time and taking it for daily walks. If you get a dog when your children are twelve or older, they may be willing and able to assume much of the responsibility for a dog's care, but you should keep an eye open to be sure the job is done, and you should be willing to help out on special occasions such as football practice or band rehearsal nights.

Should You Get a Puppy?

First, decide if you want a puppy or an older dog. You will have no way of assessing a very young puppy's inherited behavior traits because a small puppy has not yet developed its personality. You can train it to become the kind of dog you want if you spend the time and effort to do it.

A popular notion is that it's best to get a puppy so the dog can grow up with the children and won't bite them. True, you can buy a very young puppy and assume that it hasn't yet learned to bite from aggression or fear, but puppies bite constantly in play. Puppies use their mouths to explore the world. They all nip and chew on their littermates in play, and they'll naturally nip and chew on your children in play. An occasional puppy demonstrates a dominant disposition as young as six weeks, and it'll nip for real if your child gets near its food. Puppies' deciduous canine teeth are sharp and pointed, capable of scratching small hands. In addition, puppies naturally jump on each other, and they'll jump on your children. While puppies are small, this isn't a problem. But if you buy a five-pound (2.3 kg) shepherd-type puppy for your four-year-old, in three or four months the dog will weigh 30 pounds (13.6 kg) and your child will still be four years old. The puppy will be very much bigger and more active than it was when you bought it, and it'll knock your child down in play. Its sharp nails will scratch small arms and legs. You'll get tired of daubing iodine and soothing wails, and your child might well become afraid of his or her own dog. When something hurts, it's hard to explain to a child that the puppy is only playing.

If your child is a toddler and you get a puppy, be prepared to supervise every moment of the interaction between the two. While the puppy is tiny, a child can hurt it without realizing it. In addition to the humane aspect of not allowing children to torment pets, a puppy that becomes afraid of children is well on its way to biting them in self-defense.

A child who is older than about five or six years can deal with a puppy's behavior much more successfully than a toddler. An older child can even help you by giving the puppy the food you've prepared, taking it outside, and brushing it, all with your supervision. Don't expect your child to assume much responsibility until he or she is at least nine or ten. Some days the child will be interested, some days not.

A puppy requires the same amount of care and training if you have children or if you don't. Neglect of a puppy because the children take up too much of your time has the same result as neglecting one for any other reason: a poorly socialized, poorly trained dog that isn't a good pet for you, your children, or anyone else. Think twice before you buy a puppy for a small child.

Choosing an Older Dog

Shelters are full of adult dogs. Many of them are calm and submissive by nature, which is what you're looking for when you buy a dog for children. True, the adult dog in a shelter might have some problems that caused it to be there in the first place, but when you find an older dog you like, get it anyway. You can correct any bad habits—other than biting—that it might have developed. You can housebreak it, you can prevent it from chewing, you can teach it to come when called. A gentle adult dog is a far

Dogs are this young artist's favorite subject.

better choice for children than the most beautiful pup in the world that is fearful or aggressive toward children. Never count on reforming a biting dog.

How can you be sure to pick out a dog that won't bite your kids? Nothing in life is certain, but there are things you can do to increase the odds that you won't get a biter. It probably would be best to look for a dog that has been relinquished to a humane society shelter instead of a dog that was a stray. You often can get a lot of information about the past of an owner-relinquished dog, but you can't get any information at all about a stray.

Go to a shelter and look around. Take your spouse, but not your children under six years old. Small children want to stick their fingers into cages. They get impatient and they get restless, and you need to take your time when you select a dog. Also, every dog barks when strange people walk into a kennel, and small children can be frightened; this is a bad way to start a child's relationship with a dog. Take your older children along if you want to, but reserve veto power if you don't like their choice.

Question the shelter staff about every dog that comes close to your ideal. Tell them you have children, and tell them their ages. What do they think of this dog? Would they buy it for their own family? What's the history of this dog? How does it act when it's handled? Does it growl at feeding time? Does it snarl at other dogs? This is important because a dog that is aggressive toward other dogs is more likely to act dominant toward children. The opinion of the shelter personnel, if it is truthful and accurate, is of more value in selecting a dog for children than anything else. Listen carefully!

Test the Dog Before You Buy

Never buy a dog that will hurt your children! This is the *only* important consideration. You must be as sure as you possibly can be that the dog you select is not a biter. When you buy a dog for yourself, you can take appropriate action to avoid a bite, but your small child cannot.

Unless you are buying a small puppy, ask to take each dog you're considering on a leash to a quiet place. Handle it yourself first, before your children are allowed to touch it.

Stroke it all over and speak kindly to it. Push down on its shoulders and hindquarters a few times. Shove it around a little bit. If the dog acts happy to have you handle it that way, try the next test.

Have someone hold the leash short while you *pick up each of its feet.* You should start with the back feet for two reasons. First, dogs usually don't resent the back feet being handled as much as they do the front ones, and second, the back feet are further from the dog's teeth, in case it does try to bite you. Squeeze the pads just a little, not enough to cause pain. If the dog ignores that, squeeze hard enough that you're sure the dog can feel it, but never any harder than you'd squeeze your own fingers. What you're actually doing is seeing how much, if anything, it takes to make that particular dog bite.

Remember, you are a stranger to this dog and the dog is in a new and frightening place, so its reaction to you isn't necessarily what its reaction will be at home. Some dogs are submissive to adults but not to children, and will accept handling from an adult that they wouldn't accept from a child. However, most dogs are very sensitive about their feet, so if it won't bite when its feet are handled, it isn't likely to bite if any other part of its body is touched. If the dog makes a lunge for your hand, or if the dog shows its teeth, you'd better get a different dog. You can't trust small children not to touch the dog somewhere it won't like, so you need a dog you can trust not to bite them when they do.

The most common response dogs make to having a foot squeezed is to try to jerk the foot away. This is an acceptable reaction if the dog doesn't snarl or try to bite. If you're really considering a particular dog, hold onto its foot, without squeezing, for about a second. If the dog still doesn't start to bite, try it with the other feet. If the dog cries or hops around on three legs but still doesn't show its teeth, let go of the foot and buy that dog—it's not likely to bite your kids.

Don't count it as trying to bite if the dog licks your hand or sniffs at it while you're holding its foot. It's just seeing what you're doing to it. Sadly, it may not be the dog's fault if it resents having its feet touched; many dogs have had rough treatment when their nails were cut, or at other times. No matter what the cause, however, you don't want to get your children chewed up.

Introducing the Dog to the Children

As soon as you get your new dog home, put it in its Safe Space and leave it alone for a few hours. Both the dog and the children have had enough excitement for a while, so let them get acquainted when both have settled down.

Keep your dog on a leash when you introduce it to a child under six. Let the child pet the dog, but keep control of the situation. After all, you really don't know much about how the dog will act. Be careful at first with food or toys, because even a dog that won't bite might grab for food and accidentally grab some fingers along with it. Don't let your children hug the dog around the neck. A dog that is suddenly restrained in this way might bite in fear, and it's teeth will be very close to your child's face. Never leave a small child alone with a strange dog. Take the child with you when you leave the room, or put the dog back in its own Safe Space. Do this for a few weeks, until you're satisfied that your new dog is trustworthy with your children.

The big problems that most people have when they get an older puppy or dog that likes children is that the dog likes them too much. The dog that gets all excited and jumps on small children is just playing, but the children can be frightened and injured. This situation calls for training, both for the children and the dog:

- Have the children sit on the floor at first, so they can't be knocked over.
- Keep the dog on a leash until it calms down.
- Teach your children not to run and yell around the dog because the dog will think they are playing and will jump on them.
- Never shriek at or hit the dog. It won't help and it will scare both the children and the dog.

Most dogs will chew up children's toys when you aren't watching.

That's just dogs' nature, so consider it an object lesson: Teach your children to pick up their things, or pick them up for them.

Dogs and the Very Young

Infants

Much has been written about giving your dog lots of affection in the presence of your new baby, so it won't be jealous or resentful. This probably is appropriate with human siblings, but of questionable value with dogs. Your dog will be curious about the new little animal in the house, but it will consider the baby exactly that: a little animal that has strange smells and makes funny sounds. It would make no difference to your dog if you had brought home a guinea pig instead of a baby; in fact, if you show the dog affection when it acts hostile toward the new baby, the dog will interpret your kind gestures as approval of its behavior. Approval and affection certainly won't correct hostility in a dog.

Let your dog look at and sniff the baby, and allow it in the baby's room *while you are there.* It's best to keep the dog out when you aren't in the room yourself; there are a lot of interesting baby things to be chewed up. You can put a couple of chairs across the bottom of the door if you want to leave it open so you can hear when the baby cries.

The Older Baby

When your baby gets to the crawling stage, supervise every moment of its interaction with the dog. Your dog might be frightened and bite if the child backs it into a corner where it can't escape. Your dog might get aggressive if the child crawls toward its toys or its food dish. Remember, your dog doesn't really understand the fact that your child is a small human; it regards it as a strange animal that makes strange sounds and moves in strange ways.

Many dogs have a strong predatory instinct and can easily regard your baby as a prey species, something to be hunted or eaten, so be cautious. Once you see that the dog isn't hostile, you can gradually allow more interaction between the two, but never take the chance that your dog will grab your child.

The Walking Stage

When children start to walk, some dogs might demonstrate a tendency to be aggressive toward them. Until then, you have been the boss and the dog has been the submissive member of the family. Now there is a new member, a small, relatively immobile member. Although your dog is submissive toward you, it might not be submissive toward your child. If it isn't, it'll growl and then bite the child if it feels challenged. Watch that your child doesn't toddle over and grab the dog. Put the feeding bowl down only at mealtime. Be careful when your child has a toy because the dog may decide it wants it.

Since your children will be too young and too small to dominate the dog, you must do it for them. If the dog growls at a child *immediately* yank the dog into the submissive position (see page 98) and verbally correct it ("NO! NO!") just as if it had growled at you. Let the dog know that you are still the boss and you will tolerate no aggression toward a child. Supervise, supervise, supervise.

This picture is purposely being painted in dark colors. It's perfectly likely that your dog will adore your children and will tolerate any amount of abuse from them. However, your toddler's face and your dog's teeth are too near the same level; never take a chance until you are absolutely certain that the dog won't hurt a child under any circumstances.

Reasons Why Dogs Bite Children

Dominance

We have already discussed one of the reasons: Your dog sees a small, weak member of the household and tries to dominate it. The dog will perceive an older child as an adult because of size, but if the dog dominates weak adults, it will, of course, dominate an older child as well.

If your dog has received correct and sufficient submission training, it won't bite you, its owner, and it won't bite anyone you have specifically worked with *while you are present* because it has been conditioned to be submissive to your wishes. When you aren't there, the dog may assert dominance over smaller, weaker members of its social group. Supervise your small children and your dogs until you are absolutely sure that nobody will get hurt in your absence.

Predatory Instinct

The second reason children get bitten is that when they run and shriek in play, the dog gets excited. Its prey-chasing instinct is triggered, which causes it to run after the children and grab them. The dog doesn't intend to kill and eat your children, but that instinct is so strong in some dogs, even in some puppies, that they can't resist chasing anything and anyone that moves fast. The answer to this one is so simple that it really doesn't need to be explained: Don't let your children run wildly around the dog.

Fear

Children don't look or act like adults. A dog that is fearful by nature will bite with less provocation than a dog that isn't afraid. If your dog is suspicious of your children, supervise their interaction until it gets used to them. Be aware that some dogs never get over their fear of strange things, and in a dog's mind, this might include children. Supervise until the children are old enough to understand that they must leave the dog alone.

The elderly especially value their canine companions.

when it can't. *It is absolutely inexcusable for an adult to allow a child to mishandle a dog.* Teach your children to be gentle and considerate of all living things. That knowledge will stay with them for life.

Dogs and Other People's Children

Most dogs become absolutely devoted to children and would never bite, and most of these dogs are equally safe with all children. Occasionally, however, a dog is so devoted to its own family and has such strong guard dog instincts that it tries to protect its own children from their playmates or even their baby-sitter. If your children wrestle or run around with their little friends, it's best to keep the dog out of the way. Nothing makes for more ill will than your dog grabbing and possibly hurting the neighbor's child.

Some dogs learn to fear children for good a reason: Children can hurt dogs, and they can hurt puppies the most. They can treat them like stuffed toys; they can pull their ears or stick fingers in their eyes. Children can pick up puppies and drop them; they can pounce on puppies when they least expect it. Just a little of this treatment will teach a puppy or dog that children are dangerous. The dog that is afraid of children will avoid them whenever it can and will bite in self-defense

Dogs, the Elderly, and the Disabled

Many households include adults with physical handicaps. If Grandma isn't steady on her feet, she could be sent flying by your rambunctious big dog—a good way for Grandma to sustain a broken hip. Also, you shouldn't blame 85-year-old Grandpa if your huge dog gets away from him when he's trying to put it outdoors on its chain. Be sure to make appropriate arrangements to prevent a disaster. Supervise Rover when Grandma is around. Leave a short chain on Rover's collar that Grandpa can snap to the chain in the yard. Every household is different, so try to picture what could go wrong and don't let it happen!

Older people and people with disabilities especially need and value pets for companionship. They should never be denied this pleasure, even though someone else might have to furnish most of the care that pets require. If you're choosing a pet for someone who is disabled, pick a dog that's placid and mature. Pick one that is not a puppy, but *never* get an old, old dog for an old, old person. Old people need no more contact than is unavoidable with the medical problems of the aged, and that includes those of their dogs.

Empathy makes everyone's life better. Having empathy means putting yourself in another person's place; it means trying to understand another person's feelings as if they were your own. Even if Grandma's dog seems like a lot of trouble for you, don't even consider getting rid of it. Think of how Grandma would miss its companionship. Think about how you'll feel when *you* are a Grandma.

Chapter Fifteen
Your New Dog and Your Other Pets

"I would love to go to a shelter and buy another dog, but Fido hates other dogs. He'd never put up with one!"

"We really want to have another child, but Junior is so possessive of us! We'd have so much sibling rivalry!"

Both of these statements have equal validity, but actually, neither of the statements have any validity at all. The couple who really wants more than one child starts another pregnancy and enrolls Junior in a children's group to learn how to be a big brother. The person who really wants more than one dog reads this chapter and goes to a shelter.

There are two major differences between bringing a new baby home from the hospital and bringing home another dog. First, Junior can be prepared for the baby, and maybe even convinced that a little brother or sister will be fun. But no matter how much you talk to Fido, he won't understand that a puppy is on its way. Second, Junior might consider his sibling to be an intruder in his own private territory, but usually he won't try to kill it. Some Fidos will.

Choose your new dog the same way you chose your old—by deciding what kind of a dog you would really like. Do you want another like the first one? A completely different type? A puppy, or a grown dog? Remember, if you work all day, an adult dog may be the best choice for you, as it will need less of your time.

Bringing Home the New Dog

Before your new dog arrives, you should make most of the same preparations you made for your first dog. If your first dog has outgrown the need to be confined in its Safe Space, you can use that Space for the newcomer, but if your old dog still uses its Space, you'll need to provide an additional one. If you suspect that your resident dog will be reluctant to accept another dog, the new Safe Space should be out of sight of the old one. Hostile dogs that can see one another will bark and snarl, thus escalating their hostility.

Introducing a new dog to your resident one usually isn't a big problem. Most dogs are not quarrelsome by nature and really enjoy the companionship of members of their own species. If given the chance, they'll sniff each other all over and then start a romp. But before you turn them loose together, it's your job to be sure that one will not harm the other.

Learning to Live Together

Most of our dogs live in isolation from members of their own species and socialize instead with humans. After puppyhood, dogs may have no experience at all in relating to other dogs. Although most dogs are friendly to others, there are some that will act extremely hostile to any newcomer. To make them coexist, you will have to understand the source of the hostility and the methods to control it.

Instinct determines how dogs react to other animals. When two dogs meet, each must decide if the other is an enemy, a rival, a mate, or a friend. Dogs make these decisions on the basis of their inherited instincts and their previous experiences with others of their own kind.

Overcoming your resident dog's instinct of territorial aggression is the biggest problem you will encounter in introducing a new dog. Almost all dogs have this instinct to some degree. Most dogs bark when

Introduce two dogs with both on-leash.

someone comes to the door. Almost every dog chases other animals out of its yard. Some dogs show territorial aggression to an exaggerated degree and try to tear all other dogs to pieces, while some dogs only sniff noses and walk away. Many dogs view other dogs as friends and playmates, and actually welcome another dog into the family.

A dog's territorial aggression is just that: aggression toward an invader of its space, not aggression toward a sexual rival. As previously discussed, neutering a dog will not reduce its territorial instinct. That's why a dog that is neutered is just as good a watchdog as a dog that is not.

Whatever the degree of territorial instinct of your old dog, you must surmount it in order to make it accept the new one. The way you will do this is to use *your* position as the boss to convince your old dog that it is not permitted to act in an aggressive manner.

Even though territorial aggression is not a direct function of sex, the age and sex of both your old dog and your new one will influence their initial interaction. Dogs reach social maturity from about 18 months to 2 years of age. Under 18 months old, a dog can be considered to be a juvenile, and all adult dogs consider a juvenile to be less of a threat to their social position.

Adult male dogs, neutered or not, are more likely to demonstrate hostility toward one another than will an adult male and a juvenile male. An adult male dog is less likely to be aggressive toward an adult female and even less likely toward a juvenile female. Two adult females will tangle more quickly than an adult female and a juvenile of either sex. If you have an adult dog of either sex that has demonstrated aggression toward other dogs, you will be wise to select as your new dog a juvenile or one of the opposite sex, even though, in the majority of cases, dogs demonstrate so little actual aggression toward each other that this need not be a major consideration.

Introducing the Dogs to Each Other

When you get a new dog, you should make plans to introduce it to your resident dog in such a way that neither will get hurt. This means that each dog should be on a leash, each leash should be held by a person strong enough to control the dog, and the introduction

should take place in a large area so that neither dog feels crowded into a defensive position.

When you bring your new dog home, it is a good idea to let it sniff, and perhaps eliminate, in the yard where your old dog is exercised. It will get the scent of your resident dog and know that another dog is in the area. After your new dog has sniffed around, you can lead it a short distance away from the house and have a friend or family member bring out your old dog, also on a leash.

If your yard is big enough, walk both dogs back and forth about 20 feet (about 6 m.) from each other, but not yet touching noses. At this point you will be able to tell if either of the dogs is aggressive: It will snarl or bark and lunge toward the other dog. Usually, the aggressor is the resident dog. The old dog is in its own territory, while the new dog feels insecure in an unfamiliar place.

Prevent Dogfights

Never allow two strange dogs to approach each other off leash until they have *repeatedly* demonstrated that they won't fight. In the excitement of a fight, dogs that ordinarily would never bite a human will grab anything within reach, and you can get bitten. For the safety of both the dogs and yourself, never let a fight get started.

If the worst happens, however, and two dogs do start to fight, it is never safe for a person to try to stop them by catching one or both by the collar. If you have something handy to throw, use it. If you can find a *long* stick, this is the only justifiable time to hit a dog; smack both of them on the flanks and yell to distract their attention from each other. Grab something like a broom to jam between the fighters.

The appropriate action for you to take toward your aggressive older dog is strong discipline. Yank on the leash and command: "Sit!" If the dog is really aggressive, it won't sit, but will continue to lunge and bark. If it does, yank again, shove the dog into a sitting position, and command: "No! No! Sit!" Enforce the sit by whatever means necessary, including holding the dog in position.

By enforcing a command ("Sit!") when the dog is agitated by the sight of another dog, you are reinforcing your position as the boss. You are showing your aggressive dog that you will not tolerate that behavior, and you are teaching it that it must obey you even when it is excited by the presence of a strange dog.

If you strike an agitated dog, you might excite it further and escalate its aggressive behavior. In severe cases, the dog's aggression might be redirected toward you. Appropriate treatment for a dog that's trying to get at another dog is restraint with a collar and leash and very firm enforcement of another command.

When the Dogs
Are Not Aggressive

If neither of the dogs demonstrates much overt aggression, you can cautiously allow them to sniff noses, and then to sniff each other all over. If they seem friendly toward each other, you can take them into the house, both still on leashes.

Once inside the house, repeat the same procedure that you did outside. Let the dogs see each other from a little distance; let them sniff each other. Now put the new dog in its Safe Space and take the leash off the old one. You can let the old dog sniff the new one in its Space, but at the first sign of a growl, put the leash back on and enforce "Sit!"

If the dogs act at all hostile to one another in the house, try to set up three or four more sessions with a helper to control one of the dogs on a leash while you hold the other. You will soon see if the dogs will get along; in the vast majority of cases, the answer is Yes. You can try taking the leash off them, one at a time, starting with the most timid one. It should take only a few days until your new dog and your old dog are buddies. Many dogs eventually become such good friends that they can occupy the same spacious Safe Space, but be sure of this before you confine them together.

If Aggression Continues

If either dog continues to lunge and snarl, you should repeat the outdoor introductory session until the dogs become less aggressive toward each other. You must handle the aggressor very firmly by its collar and leash, but you must never strike either of the dogs. In extreme cases, these introductory sessions will have to be repeated outdoors several times a day for quite a few days; in between sessions, take each dog individually to its Safe Space and do not allow them to see each other until the next session.

Dogs are more likely to accept each other outdoors than in the smaller confines of the house, so be careful the first time you take the leashes off indoors. If one of the dogs continues to display aggression, you should continue to keep the leash on it when it is in the presence of the other dog. You must correct it by enforcing a stationary behavior ("Sit!" or "Down!") until it realizes that it must obey you even when it would like to grab the other dog. Eventually, your position of dominance will convince the dog that, under no circumstances, is it to attack the other, at least while you're around. This may take a couple of weeks of twice-daily sessions, but if you are persistent, it will happen. Remember, never leave two hostile dogs alone to start a battle when you aren't there. Separate them until you are completely sure of their behavior toward one another.

What can you do if you have nobody to hold one of the dogs during the initial introductory process? Put the newcomer in its Safe Space, let the other dog see and smell it, and enforce restrictive commands ("Sit" or "Down") even if the resident dog shows nothing but curiosity about the new one. Then fasten the new dog on a short chain in the yard, even if it's fenced, and bring out your resident dog on a leash. Have your new dog sniff it, discipline it for any show of aggression, and proceed just as though the chained dog was being held on a leash by a friend. When you take the two dogs into the house, chain the new one (close its leash in a door) before you lead in the resident one. You can do it by yourself, but it's a little harder.

Most Dogs Like Each Other

All this talk about reducing inter-dog aggression by such maneuvers as showing the old dog extra affection in the presence of the new one is just that—talk. If your new dog resents the presence of an interloper, the quickest way, almost the only way, to make it tolerate a new dog is to show the old dog that you are the boss and you aren't going to stand for that behavior. You can't let aggressive dogs fight it out without risking serious damage to one or both, and you can't keep them apart until they get used to each other, because they won't; they'll bide their time until they can use their teeth on each other.

Fortunately, most of the problems involved with introducing your new dog to your old one will be very minor, as most dogs will accept another very quickly. Your big problem might be preventing them from romping through the house at full speed and scattering furniture and small children in their wake.

Competition Between Dogs

Even if dogs are friends, each dog should always be fed in a place where it doesn't feel that it has to protect its food from another animal. It's best by far to feed each dog in its own Safe Space. If you decide to feed in separate corners of the kitchen, you'll have to remain present to prevent the dominant dog from gobbling its dinner and then fighting the other dog over its food. Unless your dogs are not in the least competitive, never use the "free choice" feeding method in which you leave dry food out in a dish for the dogs to help themselves. If you do, you might end up with one fat dog and one very thin one. A common water dish is okay as long as it is not located where either dog is fed. If it is, the dog that is fed at that place may keep the other dog away from the area and also away from the water bowl.

Dogs play with toys mainly with their mouths. To a dog, a toy is a surrogate for food. Until you are sure that your dogs won't fight, pick up all the toys, and give them to the dogs only in their Safe Spaces or when only one dog is present. Eventually, you will be able to leave toys out, but until you know the dogs won't compete, eliminate any object they might fight over.

Protect Your Puppy

Adult dogs will usually accept a puppy without much fuss, but don't leave them together for an instant unless you're absolutely sure the puppy won't pester the older dog and earn a disciplinary bite. Keep toys and food picked up, as the puppy may try to grab something the dog wants and get bitten for it. People have sometimes returned home only to find that their seemingly friendly dog has seriously attacked or even killed their new pup.

Changes in Social Position

If you bought a puppy and your adult dog accepted it, don't be surprised if they are no longer such good friends when the puppy becomes mature. As a juvenile, the puppy deferred to the older dog, and accepted its lower social position in the pack. With maturity, your puppy might challenge your other dog or dogs for boss status. You must not let them fight it out, since there is a serious risk that one will injure or even kill the other.

Be sure the bigger dog won't harm the smaller.

You can elevate the social position of one dog by taking its side against the other. You can enforce the aggressor to "Sit, Stay!" while the other dog is allowed to roam. This will work in your presence, but not in your absence. If you are firmly the boss, the dogs won't fight while you are there, but when you aren't around, they will compete to see who is second-in-command, so you must keep them apart when you aren't present. Eventually, an equilibrium usually is established by the dogs themselves. Until this happens, separate them.

Roaming Dogs

No dog should *ever* run loose without supervision, but there are some dogs that are real homebodies and never leave the yard. If you have one of these rare animals and you get another dog, don't think the first will keep the other at home. In fact, the exact opposite will happen, and the first dog will accompany the second in its wandering. Dogs, after all, are pack animals and they like companionship. If you chain the new one, the other might stay at home with it, but if you don't, they will both be gone.

Dogs on Chains

Never chain two dogs where there is the slightest chance that their chains could become entangled. Dogs have choked to death or been seriously injured when this happens. And even dogs that are the best of friends might bite each other when tangled together because they don't understand why they can't get apart. They are frightened and can mistake the restriction of the chain as an attack by the other dog.

Mounting Behavior

Dogs have two kinds of mounting actions. The most common is mating behavior. You'll be surprised to see that all dogs might do it— males, females, spayed, neutered, puppies, and adults. In this kind of mounting behavior, one dog jumps up and wraps its front legs around the other's "waist." Males might do it to males, females to males, females to other females—any two dogs. Many dogs try to mount other animals, such as cats. Some dogs try to mount humans' arms and legs, especially children's. Some dogs mount inanimate objects such as sofa cushions. Although this behavior occurs in all dogs, it is more frequent in mature dogs that are not surgically altered. In nature, the action would be a male mounting a female in heat and would result in an actual mating.

In altered pet dogs, mounting is simply a residual instinct, and not a very strong one. There's nothing wrong with a dog that mounts; it's just acting like a dog. Mounting is considered by human observers to be very impolite, so if you don't like it, just tell your dogs to do something else: "No! No! Sit!." If they persist, get firm about it. Grab the mounter and give it a little shake while you enforce the sit. It is easier to stop a dog from mounting arms and legs than from mounting another animal. If it mounts another animal, give the dog a *big* shake and a loud "growl." You're the boss, and you don't like that! Watch the dog and correct it every time, and it will soon give up trying to mount.

The other kind of dogs' mounting behavior has to do with dominance, not sex, and doesn't even look like mating activity. The dominant dog jumps up and puts its front paws on the shoulders or back of the other dog, usually just for a second or two. The "top" dog is expressing its physical superiority to the other one and it is trying to place the "bottom" dog in a submissive position.

This behavior is often seen in play, and occasionally as a preluce to a fight between two dogs. If your dogs do this without growling at each other, it's harmless, but if one or both growls, they may fight.

Dogs and Cats

It's supposed to be traditional for cats and dogs to fight, but in actuality, they don't really fight. In most cases, it's the dog attacking the cat and the cat that can't escape defending itself with tooth and claw. Even though domestication has eliminated dogs' need to hunt for food, it has not eliminated their instinct to chase animals of other species. This instinct—prey aggression—is most likely to be strongest

"Like dogs and cats!"

in the hunting breeds and large dogs in general.

If you have a cat and then get a dog or have a dog and then get a cat, you'll want to teach them to coexist without damage to either. This is easily done if you have an adult cat and get a puppy. A dog introduced to cats as a pup usually learns to regard them as fellow beings, even friends. If a puppy gets too rough with a cat, it'll receive appropriate discipline—from the cat! One scratched nose usually teaches a pup not to mess with hostile felines. Owners have to be somewhat careful about the eyes of small pups and small breed dogs, however. If your resident cat is really fierce, keep your puppy away from its claws.

When you bring a puppy into the house, most resident adult cats will hiss and stay out of its way for at least a few days. Some cats will seem to spend weeks on top of the refrigerator every time the puppy is allowed in the kitchen. Don't worry—eventually the cat will come down. Be sure, however, that the puppy doesn't frighten the cat away from its food or its litter box. A cat too timid to get to its "bathroom" will pick another spot to eliminate, and it's likely to be on a corner of the Oriental rug.

If you have an adult dog and get a kitten, protect the kitten. Dogs can do a lot of damage to a tiny kitten, even if they are only playing. Kittens need their own Safe Spaces too. When the kitten gets big enough to run and climb, your dog and your cat may even play together, but supervise all interaction between the two while the cat is very small.

Some dogs can never be trusted with cats. Many dogs that have reached adulthood without any contact with cats will always regard them as a prey species, something to be chased and killed. You can control such a dog's behavior *while you are present* in the same way you taught your old dog to tolerate your new one, by being the boss and not permitting the dog to get near the cat. However, if you aren't in the room to influence the dog, a really aggressive one may kill your cat if it can catch it. Don't take a chance; keep them apart. Besides

damage to the cat, your house may end up in a shambles by the time your dog gets the cat off the top of the curtains.

Don't be surprised if your cat and your dog are the best of friends in the house, but your dog chases the cat when it sees it outside. This is the prey instinct in action: When the dog sees a moving animal, it chases it. Most of the time, the dog won't actually hurt a cat it knows, but the cat doesn't realize that, so it runs. That's the self-preservation instinct in action, and it's a good idea from the standpoint of the cat; some dogs are fine with cats indoors and will kill them outside.

Dogs and Small Pets

Rabbits, hamsters, and guinea pigs all look like prey species to dogs, and with good reason. Dogs' wild ancestors feasted on just such animals, and our pets still have the instinct to have them for lunch. There are dogs that coexist happily with all other animals, even mice, but these are not common. It's always advisable to prevent contact between your dogs and all small pets, including reptiles such as snakes and iguanas, which you wouldn't think dogs would regard as prey.

Birds in their cages seem to be especially attractive as prey to dogs, probably because birds seem to be in nearly constant motion. A dog that knocks over a bird cage can smash its occupant as well as the cage, and a bird that is not injured by the falling cage can harm itself with its frantic fluttering to escape. It's wise to place all birds' cages high enough to be out of reach of your dogs. Suspend the cages from the ceiling rather than relying on post-type cage stands that are easily upset.

Dogs are usually the aggressors in dog-bird confrontations, but don't disregard the real possibility that some of the larger parrot species will bite chunks out of your curious dog. Even parrots that are very tame toward humans are often afraid of dogs and will bite fiercely to defend themselves. Parrots also express territorial dominance; many is the dog that has been driven from its owner's side by a large, jealous macaw.

Parrots are wasteful feeders, and many dogs relish the bits of food that larger pet birds toss out of their cages. If your dog is one of these, be careful not to give your parrot large nuts or sharp shells that can harm your dog's intestines.

Dogs and Large Animals

Dogs running loose in rural areas can, of course, cause a lot of damage to livestock. In fact, the original reason for dog licensing was to provide money to reimburse farmers for sheep or chickens killed by dogs. According to the law governing ani-

This blue heeler romps with her owner's goat.

mal behavior, owners are always liable for any damage done by their dogs, and must pay for killed or injured stock if it can be proven that their dogs were at fault. Also, any owners of livestock are permitted by law to kill by any means any and all dogs that attack their stock on property they own, rent, or lease. This means that if your dogs run loose in a rural area and harm any other animals, you will have to pay. It also means that your dogs can be legally killed by anyone whose animals they molested or who claims that their animals were molested. The bottom line is: *Never* let your dogs run loose without supervision, even if you live on a farm.

There's another reason to keep your dogs away from livestock: Horses and cattle don't always run from dogs. Many large animals, horses especially, will not only stand their ground, but are aggressive toward dogs and will chase, stomp, and kick those that invade their pastures. Most horse owners are also dog owners and keep their dogs under control or train them to stay away from horses. Dog-owning neighbors of horse owners might not recognize the risk, and dogs that have never seen horses might regard them as something to chase. Many a dog has been horribly injured or killed by a neighbor's horse or pony.

Obviously, the way to keep your dogs from chasing horses is the same way you keep them from chasing cats: confinement and discipline. Don't think that your dog will get "just a little kick" and become afraid to get near horses. A horse is a large animal, and a little kick can kill a dog. As we've said over and over: Be vigilant and supervise!

Chapter Sixteen

Housebreaking: The Mess and How to Avoid It

The big question asked by every prospective owner is: "Is it housebroken?" The fate of many dogs hangs in the balance. If it's housebroken, it gets a new home. If it's not, it goes to the shelter. Failure to housebreak is one of the most common reasons dogs are relinquished, and in virtually every instance, the dog doesn't have a problem; the dog is just acting like a dog, but it's the owners who have the problem. The owners have failed to take advantage of natural canine instincts to keep their dog from messing where it shouldn't.

Housebreaking Is a Natural Act

Dogs' elimination behavior is controlled entirely by habit. When a dog, any dog of any age, goes into a new home, all its habits are disrupted because it is in a new environment. If your new shelter dog's card had "yes" next to "housebro-

ken," don't assume the dog will never mess in your house. In the first place, that "yes" might be only a former owner's attempt to make his or her dog more adoptable. In the second place, housebroken means different things to different people. To you it might mean a dog that would rather die than mess in the house; to someone else, it might mean a dog that doesn't mess unless you're not looking its way. To a dog, housebroken means that it has the opportunity to eliminate as its habits dictate—at its regular time and in its regular place. When a dog goes into a strange new household, it no longer has that opportunity. A formerly housebroken dog might not act housebroken at all.

Start training every dog you get as though it was never housebroken, and you soon will have a dependable dog. If the dog has already been trained to be clean in someone's house, it will learn to be clean in your house in a few days. It's easy to housebreak adult dogs

Always start housebreaking your new dog on a leash.

because they are old enough to have bowel and bladder control; therefore, many that were never housebroken will be trained within a week. Puppies will be housebroken as soon as they are physically capable of controlling their bowels and bladder. Housebreaking will take place without the yelling and scrubbing and all the other trauma often associated with the process. It will be done by establishing in the dog's mind the habit of eliminating only in the place you have chosen.

Positive Housebreaking

Your dog has to urinate. Your dog has to defecate. These are natural, unavoidable actions. You can't teach your dog not to do it, but you *can* teach your dog to do it in the right place. *Don't* start by punishing your dog for messing indoors; that's a negative approach. Start by teach-

ing your dog to mess outside in the place you've selected—that's positive housebreaking.

Training books tell you to watch your dog in the house, and the minute it squats, yell at it and take it outside. This is training your dog backward, because by the time it squats, it's too late—the dog has selected a spot and initiated the action. All it learns by being grabbed and yelled at is to avoid humans when it has to eliminate. Besides that, some dogs, especially puppies, can't shut off the action once they've started, so you'll end up carrying a urinating dog while dashing for the door. It's easier to clean up one place on the floor than your pants and the entire hallway.

Start Housebreaking the Right Way

Before you even get the dog, have two things prepared.

1. Select a place that will be the permanent "bathroom." An area in the yard of about ten feet (3 m) square will be sufficient. (If you are an apartment dweller and decide to paper-train your dog, pick out an area the size of about four unfolded sheets of newspaper.) If you can, choose a place that's easy to clean up, such as on a concrete driveway. Fecal material is hard to pick off grass, but if your new dog is accustomed to using grass as its bathroom, it'll prefer to continue that habit. Select an area close to an outside door as you're going to

be spending time standing out there in all kinds of weather.

2. Construct your new dog's private Safe Space before you bring it home. Remember, this can be a cage, a pen, or whatever your situation dictates, but it must be a secure enclosure.

As soon as you take your new dog out of the car, take it to its bathroom area *on a leash* if it's an adult or a big puppy. Carry it there and set it down if it's just a little puppy. Even if you have a fenced yard, keep the dog on a leash so that you can keep it in the small area. You want to establish the habit of eliminating in the selected spot from the start. Stand there for a few minutes to see if your new friend will use the bathroom area. You can say, "Hurry up," or whatever term you use for elimination. If the dog urinates or defecates, you've got half the battle won. If it does or if it doesn't, when you take it into your house for the first time, put it in its Safe Space *immediately.* Give it a drink of water and go away. Let the dog have a chance to settle down in its new home. If it whines or barks, turn on the television so you can't hear it.

In an hour or two, come back and snap on the leash. Take the dog back to the bathroom area. Stand there and hope the dog eliminates. If it doesn't, take it back to its Safe Space. It is *very important* that the first place the dog uses to relieve itself is the area you have selected. You must establish the habit of using that area and only that area for the bathroom.

Eventually, your new dog will do one of two things: It will either eliminate in the area you've selected, or it will eliminate in its own Safe Space. If if it does it in the Safe Space, take the dirty papers outside and put them in the bathroom area, with a rock on them so they won't blow away. The dog will smell its own elimination and will be more likely to do it there the next time.

When it is time to feed your new dog, take it back out to the bathroom. Then feed the dog in its own Safe Space. As soon as the dog has eaten, take it back to the bathroom area. You can't just let the dog out into the yard without going out with it, because it's important that you know if it has eliminated. You'll get tired of standing there, chanting, "Hurry up, Hurry up," but it will train your dog in the quickest and most positive way possible. As soon as your dog eliminates, you can allow it freedom in the house, but watch it: If the dog sniffs around as though its looking for a bathroom spot, take it out again. Puppies are much more likely to do this than older dogs. Any time you can't pay attention to your new dog, put it back in its Safe Space.

Good Habits Develop Quickly

It won't be long until your dog urinates and defecates in its bathroom area almost as soon as you take it there. In fact, this will happen almost immediately if you've bought

This small dog has learned to be housebroken, so it is allowed out without the leash.

an older dog that has already been housebroken. If you've bought an adult dog that never lived in a house, it will learn almost as quickly, as these dogs are used to eliminating outdoors and will continue to do so.

Some dogs take much more time sniffing around before they will eliminate. If your dog is a slow one and you don't give it a long enough opportunity to urinate and defecate, you will defeat your own purpose. The dog has to do it—if it doesn't get the chance to do it where you want it to, it'll do it where you don't want it to. Put on your coat and hat and control your impatience.

Housebreaking the Puppy

Would you punish your baby for wetting its diaper? Of course not. You'd just change him or her until your child is old enough to be toilet trained. When the child is old enough, would you punish him or her for a mistake? Certainly not. You'd teach him how to use the potty. A little puppy is no different from a little child. If you get a puppy older than six weeks, it is ready for potty training.

A puppy hasn't formed any habits, so you have to teach it what to do. By taking it to the bathroom area *immediately* every time you take it out of its Safe Space, you will soon get it into the habit of eliminating outside. Carry a very small puppy so it doesn't stop to eliminate on the way out, and stand there until it eliminates. You're teaching it to use the "potty," and not to mess its "diaper" (its Safe Space). Both children and puppies will make mistakes, but eventually, both will learn.

Stay with Your Dog Outside

There are three reasons for your staying at the bathroom area with your dog on a leash:

1. You need to know if it has eliminated so you can safely let it loose in the house.
2. You want to keep the dog in a small area and not let it roam around, so the dog will learn to associate that area with prompt performance. If you let it roam and sniff, it will take much longer for it to decide to eliminate. If you restrict it to a small area, it will learn to eliminate almost as soon as it gets there.
3. When you take your dog visiting, you'll want it to be comfortable eliminating on-leash. Seldom are there places you can turn your dog

loose to select its own spot. Be assured that you won't have to stand outside with your dog on a leash forever, just until you get it trained.

Establish a regular schedule with your dog: outside first thing in the morning; again after breakfast; at noon if you're not at work and as soon as you get home if you are; after dinner; before bedtime. When your dog regularly eliminates outside, you can allow it more and more freedom in the house.

Accidents

If you've established in your dog the strong habit of eliminating in its spot outside, it will make very few mistakes. Dogs are such creatures of habit that one that is trained to eliminate in one area outside is very likely to show great distress, whine, and run to the door if it has to urinate or defecate and can't get to its customary area.

If your dog that routinely is using its outside area does make a mistake in the house and you *catch it when it starts,* you can growl fiercely ("NO! NO!") and even give it a little shake. Let it know you don't like that. If you think it's not finished, take it outside. If the dog messes in the house and you find it *even five seconds later,* just clean it up. Keep your temper—it's too late to punish. Punishment will not teach the dog not to do that, because you'll be punishing when the dog is no longer messing. Even

seconds late, the dog can't mentally connect the act with the punishment. All you'll accomplish with late punishment is to frighten and confuse the dog since it won't know the meaning of the punishment.

If your dog, even your young puppy, messes in the house more than very occasionally, it's your fault, as you have not sufficiently strengthened the habit of using only the designated bathroom area. Go back to the beginning of housebreaking. Return the dog to its Safe Space unless you have seen it eliminate outside and unless you can watch its actions in the house.

When can you allow your dog full freedom in the house? You'll know when that time comes. Your dog will eliminate in its outside area as soon as it gets there. If you have a fenced yard, you no longer have to go out with it, you just open the door. The dog wants to eliminate in the right place because it has established the habit of doing it there. It doesn't want to eliminate anywhere else, and that includes inside your house.

If Things Go Wrong

Nothing is perfect and no two dogs are exactly alike, so positive housebreaking won't work perfectly all the time. The most common problem is the dog that messes in its Safe Space. Every dog training book states, correctly, that dogs do not like to dirty their own beds. The books tell you to make their enclosures small enough so that if they do mess in them, they'll have to lie in it. But just as dogs become accustomed to using one spot outside, some will become used to with living with their own waste. Some dogs seem not to care. These dogs are not basically "dirty" animals; they have learned to do this because they have been confined to their Safe Space at the times when their normal elimination behaviors occur.

If you work full time and your dog consistently eliminates in its own enclosure, you might have to put up with it. Just think about how many times a day you go to the bathroom. Even though your dog doesn't snack and drink coffee all day, it can't keep from eliminating if it is confined too long. If this is your situation, make your dog's Safe Space bigger, not smaller. Put its bed in half of it and newspapers in the other half. You will have, in effect, a dog that is trained to the outside when it can get there and paper-trained when it can't.

Another remedy for the dog that consistently messes in its Safe Space is to try to change the time it would naturally eliminate to the time when you are able to take it out. Food stays in a dog's digestive system on an average of ten to twelve hours. If you don't believe this, feed your dog some dog biscuits that contain red dye and watch to see when its stool is reddish from the food coloring. Adult dogs are usually fed once or twice a day. If the dog has a bowel movement first thing in the morning, it will contain the remains of the food it was fed for dinner the previous night. If it has a bowel movement before bedtime, it will be the food it had for breakfast. If your dog has a lot of food for breakfast, it will have a big bowel movement at bedtime *or* during the night. If it has a big dinner, it will have a big movement in the morning *or* during the day.

If your dog messes in its space during the night, try feeding it most of its food in the evening. Give it only a little breakfast if you want to feed twice a day, so that its major bowel movement will be in the morning when you are there to take it outside.

If your dog messes in its Safe Space while you are away during the day, feed it its big meal in the morning. That food will result in the bowel movement the dog has at night after you've returned home to take it out.

Dogs' systems vary in the speed with which they digest food, so this plan won't always work perfectly, but it certainly will help. It might take several days of altering the size of your dog's meals to see the results.

The other problem dog that messes in its Safe Space is the one that has formed the habit of doing it, and not formed the habit of eliminating outside. This dog has its signals crossed, and thinks the Safe Space is the bathroom and the yard is the place to play. This is the dog that will play around for hours outside and mess as soon as you put it back in its pen. You'll have to do a little work to retrain a dog that has developed this habit.

Take the dog outside. Stand there. If the dog doesn't eliminate, take it back in, put it in its Space, leave the leash on, and *wait right there* until the dog squats. Grab it before it can defecate and take it back out. If it still doesn't defecate outside, repeat the same thing: Take it back to its Space and wait until it squats; then grab the leash and take it back out before it has a chance to move its bowels. Eventually, the dog will have to defecate outside. You'll have to do this several days in a row, maybe several times a day, but sooner or later the dog will learn to eliminate when it gets outside and not wait until it gets back in.

A variation of this problem is the dog that is seemingly housebroken but sneaks into another room when you're not looking to move its bowels. This behavior is common in dogs that have been housebroken backwards. They have been punished for messing in the house so they are afraid to defecate in your sight. The solution is to not let the dog sneak away. Keep taking it out to the correct bathroom area until it performs, and if it doesn't, put it back in its own Space and take it out again later. Don't ever let it loose in your house until you've actually seen it eliminate outside.

Scent Marking

Unneutered male dogs, and the occasional female, will urinate in very small amounts in many places in the house. The dog that does this is marking its territory with the scent of its urine, as discussed in Chapter 12. This behavior is strongly sex-related and only weakly dominance-related. Even dogs that are submissive to humans and other dogs will scent mark, although they will usually do less of it than will a dominant dog. If you have two unneutered dogs, both will scent mark, not only the dominant one. Each dog will lift its leg where the other dog did it. It becomes a sort of a scent marking contest.

The dog that scent marks is not doing it because it has to urinate, so rushing it outside to teach it "where to go" won't have any effect. In fact, dogs often lift their legs and go through the motions of scent marking after their bladders are completely empty. Dogs prefer to mark upright objects like furniture and draperies, just as their canine ancestors marked the bushes and trees in their home territories to warn away intruders.

Neutering (occasionally spaying) is the most effective method to prevent scent marking. A puppy that is neutered before puberty will rarely learn to mark even if it lives in a household with a dog that does scent mark. A dog neutered after it has developed the habit might continue to mark for weeks or months after surgery, but eventually the behavior is extinguished because the neutered dog lacks the hormones that cause it. Only very occasionally will a dog that was neutered when it was mature scent mark for the rest of its life. Once in a while, a dog that is a confirmed marker stops entirely as soon as it has the surgery.

For a dog of any age, neutering is the first and only really effective method of minimizing or eliminating scent marking, although verbal correction will help. If you yell often enough, your dog probably will learn not to mark when you're around. Unless you don't mind smelly yellow upholstery and draperies, it's best to confine the scent marker to its own Space when you're not there or until it gets over the habit.

Can all dogs be housebroken? The answer is a qualified "Yes." A few dogs will never be completely trustworthy, and they will always need to be confined to their Safe Spaces

when their owners are away, but this is not a big problem. The correct use of the Safe Space entirely eliminates dog messes in the house.

Positive Housebreaking Works!

Never try to housebreak your dog backward. Never use negative training by punishing it for eliminating in the wrong place. Instead, use positive training by first teaching it to eliminate in the right place. Then prevent it from making mistakes by confining it in its Safe Space when you can't supervise its actions. Sooner than you think, your dog will mess *only* outside.

With positive housebreaking, without punishment, and often without a single spot on the rug, your dog will be housebroken. Now, wasn't that easy?

Chapter Seventeen
Chewing, Jumping, and Barking

Believe it or not, some people actually give up wonderful dogs for very trivial reasons. Dogs that chew table legs, dogs that devour carpeting, dogs that get muddy footprints on Aunt Tillie's new white slacks—these unfortunate animals often end up at shelters, even though these problems are not the dogs' fault and are easily prevented or corrected. When you find the right dog at a shelter, even though it has a history of chewing or jumping, buy it. This sort of "bad" behavior is insignificant and easily corrected. The dog that chews, the dog that jumps, the dog that barks may be exactly the dog you want. Although its former owner gave up on it rather than prevent or correct its "bad" behavior, you can make such a dog the pet you want with only a little time and effort. It will be well worth it.

Chewing

It is natural for a dog to chew. All young dogs and many older ones do it. Dogs are carnivores. They evolved from animals that had to catch and eat other animals in order to survive. Since we provide the food for our domestic dogs, they don't have to hunt to eat, but the mind of the domestic dog is still programmed to actively chase and seize prey with their jaws.

Dogs are active; dogs are intelligent; dogs are curious. Our pet dogs have no activity that takes the place of their ancestors' need to constantly hunt for food. So the reason dogs chew is simple: They crave activity and they have nothing else to do!

Human psychologists would say that dogs are fixated at the oral stage. Dogs explore and investigate objects with their mouths. A wild dog would be discovering if the object is good to eat. The domestic dog is simply obeying its instincts when it chews your shoes and the legs of your couch. It doesn't intend to do harm; it is just acting like an animal that instinctively wants to do something with its mouth.

When does a dog destroy household furnishings? When nobody is around to stop it, of course. "But I give it lots of its own toys! Why does it chew my things?" A dog thinks like a dog; it doesn't think like a person. A dog doesn't know the difference between its own things and your things that are within its reach. If you provide lots of dog toys, it will chew on them until it gets bored. It will chew on meat-scented toys for quite a while, often until the object is destroyed, then it will look around for something else to occupy its attention, and that something else might be your antique chair.

Why doesn't the dog destroy things in your presence? Obviously because you're there to tell it "No, bad dog," and hand it one of its own toys. If you were completely engrossed in a TV program and paying no attention to the dog, you might find that it chewed the table leg right beside you. Your presence alone doesn't always deter it from chewing unless you are occupying its attention.

Chewing Out of Spite

That dogs chew things out of malice or spite toward their owners is another common old wives' tale. Dogs don't get "mad" at their owners and destroy household furnishings out of "spite" because they're left alone. To apply these human emotions to dogs is pure *anthropomorphism,* or assigning human traits to an animal. Fortunately, spite is simply beyond dogs' mental capacities. While it's true that dogs that are accustomed to constant companionship don't like it when they are left alone, they chew because they get bored, not because they get mad.

You've read about training your dog not to chew the wrong things. You've heard about hot pepper, about verbal and physical punishment, about other forms of *aversion conditioning,* which involves making a dog afraid to do something. Forget it. It doesn't work very well in preventing chewing, and it surely won't work well enough to insure that your dog won't destroy something you value. Why take chances? There is a 100-percent guaranteed way to keep your dog from destroying anything, and it is very simple. Don't give your dog the opportunity to chew up your belongings; pick up your shoes and teach your children to put away their toys.

Using the Safe Space

Put your dog in its Safe Space every time you go away. Remember, that's why it's called a Safe Space: The dog is safe and your home is safe. Eventually, you might find that your mature dog has lost most of its desire to chew and you can then begin to trust it. Older dogs often chew only on toys they really like, which is another reason to consider buying a dog that's not still a puppy.

Confinement or Isolation Anxiety

Most dogs that chew when alone are just suffering from boredom and seeking something to do with their mouths. They might pace around a little bit, take a nap, play with their toys, then look for something else to occupy their attention. That's when they rip the stuffing out of the couch. These chewers are normal dogs with nothing else to do.

Dog behaviorists love the term *separation anxiety.* They use it to imply that a dog chews household objects when alone only because the dog is so devoted to its owners that it becomes frantic when separated from them, or that the former shelter dog is terrified that its beloved owners will never return. This is anthropomorphism at best, and is seldom a valid assumption. If you want proof, notice that the presence of any person, even a stranger, will prevent the chewing behavior of a dog that chews from boredom.

The rare dog that acts "crazy" when alone is probably suffering from *confinement anxiety* or from *isolation anxiety.* These dogs have an abnormal aversion to being locked up or to being alone. When locked alone in a room or in a Safe Space, such a dog will leap around, pace wildly, bark or howl, claw at the door, shred upholstery, pant until it froths at the mouth, urinate and defecate without control. This behavior will occur within a few minutes after the dog is isolated, not an hour or more later when the normal dog has had time to become bored with its surroundings. A few dogs will show this

behavior even if confined to a cage when their owner is nearby. The slang term for this is 'stir crazy." These dogs didn't get stir crazy from being kept in a small space. Usually they got that way from never experiencing confinement at all. When they find themselves locked in, they become frantic to escape. Attempts to alter the behavior of a dog with true confinement anxiety usually involves confining the dog for gradually increasing periods of time. If the dog is truly abnormal, this technique is unlikely to succeed unless some sort of tranquilizers are used when the dog is first confined.

A less severe form of confinement anxiety is shown by the dog that whirls around and around in its Safe Space, or by the dog that paces in its Space from one side to another like a bear in a cage. Most of these dogs whirl or pace only when they get excited, at mealtime, for example. This type of anxiety is not serious if the dog does it infrequently, as these dogs don't harm themselves or anything else.

Fortunately, you're never going to buy a shelter dog with serious confinement anxiety, because shelter dogs are kept in cages, so you can detect if a shelter dog has this problem and you won't buy it. Don't mistake confinement anxiety for a dog that's glad to see you and jumps around wagging its tail. The friendly dog looks happy, while the anxious dog looks crazy. The friendly dog stops jumping to lick your hand when you approach. The anxious dog cannot stop its actions until it drops from exhaustion, and it resumes its actions as soon as it catches its breath. Remember: True confinement anxiety is not common in dogs, and true separation anxiety may not even exist.

Noise Anxiety

A fairly common (and real) mental aberration in dogs is *noise anxiety.* Dogs with this problem are the ones that crawl under the bed at the first sound of thunder, that try to run away from the child with the cap pistol, or tremble violently when a car backfires. These dogs are likely to be perfect when alone in the house—until it starts to rain. They have learned to associate the sound of rain with the sound of thunder, which is intolerable to them. Sometimes, dogs with noise anxiety appear to be able to predict the weather. They start to tremble and act strange long before it starts to rain. It is theorized that these dogs detect the differences in barometric pressure or ozone levels that precede a storm.

Dogs with noise anxiety get frantic. They may run and hide somewhere or urinate and defecate without control. Many dogs with severe noise anxiety tear up whatever they can reach. This kind of destruction is called *displacement activity* or *redirected aggression;* the dog cannot attack the source of its fear, so it attacks something else. The only appropriate way to avoid having your house wrecked if you have a dog like this is to confine your dog in its Safe Space whenever you're not at home and it might start to rain.

Noise anxiety is a big problem with some dogs. Owners who attempt to comfort their dogs with soothing words only reinforce in the dogs' minds the idea that their fearful behavior is appropriate. Unfortunately, many dogs that exhibit noise anxiety do not develop the behavior until they are mature, and get worse as they get older. *Counterconditioning,* a procedure in which the dog is very gradually exposed to louder and louder noises while it is doing something pleasant such as eating, has been used to try to help these dogs overcome their fear. Counterconditioning for noise anxiety is complicated and generally unsuccessful. Tranquilizers are sometimes more successful, but it's hard to predict when they'll be needed, except for the Fourth of July.

Warning: Consult your veterinarian before you give human tranquilizers to dogs, as some human drugs will kill dogs.

Jumping

Poor Aunt Tillie! Her white slacks are ruined. Poor Junior! Flat on his back, wailing his little lungs out. Poor Rover! Confused and frightened by everyone yelling at him, waving their arms, and smacking him with the leash. Let's avoid all this. Let's teach Rover to keep all four feet on the ground.

Jumping on people is not an easy activity to eliminate. It involves every person the dog encounters and every time and place the dog encounters any person. The usual way to teach a dog *not* to do something is to make it very unpleasant when it does it. Teaching a dog *not* to jump on people involves painful and frightening things, like smashing it with your knee or stomping on its back feet. Why give your dog the idea that it will receive pain when it comes near you? Even if you smash and stomp until Rover won't jump on you, it will still jump on other people. Aunt Tillie and little Junior won't be as adept at smashing and stomping as you are. Don't try to teach your dog not to jump on people; teach it to do something else instead of jumping.

In its whole life, a dog really needs to obey only two commands: "Come" and "Sit," and you'll use "Sit" to teach your dog not to jump. In speaking to your dog, the command "Sit" really means "Sit-Stay." It means the dog is supposed to assume a sitting position and stay there until it hears your release command. Most people use "Okay" as a release, but you can use whatever you want as long as you use the same word every time. Some trainers add the command "Stay," but this is using two words where one is better. Think about it: Do you ever say "Sit" to your dog when you don't intend it also to stay?

Even Aunt Tillie can say, "Sit" effectively, and once Rover obeys the command, the jumping problem is solved. When the muddy dog rushes toward her, she speaks firmly: "Rover, Sit!" The dog sits immediately, wagging and squirming with delight at seeing a friend. Aunt Tillie rubs its head, and says: "Good dog, good dog!" Everyone is happy except the dry cleaner.

The "Sit" Command

"Sit" is the easiest command you will ever teach your dog. All training books tell you how to teach it, but you don't even need a book. All you do is hold the dog by the collar (or

This dog has learned to sit on command.

a short leash) with one hand and push it into a sitting position with the other hand while giving the command: "Sit!" If your dog gets up before you say "Okay," you push it back down and repeat: "Sit!" Your dog will learn it in a few days, some dogs in only one or two five-minute lessons. You can give a mini-lesson many times a day, and your dog will learn "Sit" even more quickly. You can apply the "Sit" command, and enforcement if needed, before feeding your dog or snapping on the leash for a walk. You can teach "Sit" at any time all day long.

There's no problem in teaching a dog to sit. The problem arises in enforcing the command when the dog is excited about something else. You have to be consistent and determined to do this. You have to enforce the command every time you utter the word, and you have to enforce it under a wide variety of circumstances. Take your dog for a walk and stop at a school yard. Then have it sit and watch the kids run around and yell. Or set the dog up for a "Sit" lesson by having friends come over. Open the door with the dog on a leash and enforce "Sit" while you greet your guests. Sooner than you think, your dog will sit and wait to be praised instead of getting footprints on everybody.

If Junior is still very small, you might have a problem with his giving the command or with Rover understanding it, but you still don't want your child to be knocked down by your dog. In this case, you'll have to be the one who gives the command and enforces it. Eventually, the dog will sit automatically whenever Junior appears. Of course, Junior might be a big boy by that time. If so, he can say "Sit" for himself.

Your seemingly perfectly trained dog will occasionally get carried away by excitement, especially when it greets you, its owner. Never consider your job as a trainer to be finished. Once in a while, you'll have to give Rover a little refresher course. Be prepared to do it, and remember: The key to success is to enforce the "Sit" command every time you say the word.

Barking

"The neighbor called again today. He said the dog barks all day long, and he's going to call the police. That dog will just have to go!"

Sound familiar? Chewing and jumping are easy problems to correct. With only a little effort, these behaviors can be controlled or eliminated from every dog. Barking is a different situation entirely.

Dogs bark for several reasons. There is the watchdog bark, the excitement bark, the play bark. Dogs bark a warning when they hear a strange noise. They bark to repel other dogs that walk past their yard. They bark near feeding time. They often bark because they are bored and dislike confinement.

A dog that barks when its owner is present is not a problem. If the

owner wants to stop it, all he or she needs to do is to give the dog another activity to replace the barking. This is another reason to teach and enforce the command, "Sit!" The dog hears a car door slam down the street and starts to bark. Instead of yelling at the dog to be quiet, which the dog won't understand since it barks because of its watchdog instinct, the owner says, "Sit." It seems that a dog can't concentrate on two things at once; it can't sit (sit-stay) and also bark unless it has been specifically trained to do both at once. When "Sit" is a strong learned behavior, the dog stops barking. Eventually, the dog sits and cocks its head at strange noises. If the noise is persistent or nearby, the watchdog instinct will override the "Sit" training. The dog will jump to its feet and bark, and the owner can go to investigate the source of the noise or stop the barking with another "Sit" command.

Nuisance Barking

Nuisance barking occurs when there is nobody there to correct the dog. Another dog for company won't stop nuisance barking, as both dogs will bark and make twice as much noise. Nuisance barking annoys everyone within earshot, and uncorrected nuisance barking has cost many a dog its happy home.

Nuisance barking is caused by one of two things. The first is the watchdog instinct. The dog alone in a house or apartment hears a noise and runs from window to window and barks. The dog in a fenced yard races along the fence and barks at everything that passes. The dog tied outside leaps to the end of its chain while making as much noise as possible. Even the dog in its Safe Space hears a footstep and starts to bark.

The second cause for nuisance barking is *confinement frustration,* sometimes called *isolation frustration.* Confinement frustration is not an abnormal dog behavior as is confinement anxiety (see page 134). Many normal dogs resent confinement. The dog that can't get loose expresses its frustration by barking or whining. Confinement frustration is shown by most puppies that cry at night until they are used to their new homes, by many adult dogs that bark and whine in their Safe Spaces, and by dogs that sit out in the yard and bark for attention.

Unless your neighbors live far away or also own barking dogs, eventually someone complains. If they complain enough, you have to do something about the noise.

You cannot eliminate nuisance barking by yourself, because when the dog actually is barking, you are not there to correct it! A dog cannot associate punishment with something it did even a few seconds in the past. To be effective, punishment must occur *at the exact same time* as the infraction, so the dog can mentally connect the two.

The barker doesn't realize that you are punishing it for barking because you are punishing it too late. When it hears you approach, it stops barking, so it is not barking when you get there to punish it. It will associate the punishment with your approach, not with the barking. Your dog will never learn to not bark when you are not around, no matter how often you run out there and swat it or yell at it.

What can you do about nuisance barking, short of earplugs or moving away from your neighbors? This depends on the situation.

At times it becomes impossible to tolerate nuisance barking, for example, if neighbors threaten to take you to court for disturbing the peace, or if your landlord decides not to renew your lease because you have a barking dog. It's not uncommon to have to make hard choices because your dog barks while you're at work: Move, quit your day job, or get rid of the dog. The first two are not often practical, and most dog-owners are horrified at the third option.

But you have to do something. Nuisance barkers won't stop if you just ignore them, since they're barking from watchdog instinct or from isolation frustration. You must take action if you are to keep your dog.

Restrict the Watchdog's Environment

The dog that runs from window to window in your house or apartment and barks at the slightest sound or movement might be deterred if it cannot run around or cannot see out of the window. Put your barker in its

Safe Space when you go away, even though it has long ago stopped messing or chewing in the house. You can try leaving a radio on; if it hears noise constantly, it might not bark at a new sound from outside.

The same treatment might work for the dog that barks out in the yard. If it's in its Safe Space, it can't see anything to bark at. If it does bark, its Space is probably indoors, so the barking won't sound so loud to the neighbors. Sometimes this works, sometimes it doesn't, but a change of environment is the first thing to try for the nuisance barking watchdog.

If your dog barks in its Safe Space the whole time you are at work, you can try giving it a bigger Space, even an entire room if you can trust it. This is often not possible, and just as often not effective. Some dogs bark if they are confined at all, even in a large yard, and owners should not be so foolish as to leave a dog loose in his house if they think it might mess all over or trash the place. You probably need another way to silence the nuisance barker.

Surgical Debarking

The debarking operation consists of the surgical removal of a portion of the dog's vocal chords. This veterinary procedure used to be common, but has now fallen into disfavor for several reasons:

1. It's major surgery and it requires general anesthesia. Bleeding is a problem. Only surgeons trained in the technique and who have special instruments can do the operation.
2. It's expensive. Debarking could cost a couple of hundred dollars. Since it is elective surgery, no animal medical insurance covers it.
3. The dog has postoperative pain, or at least discomfort, equal to or greater than the pain of a tonsillectomy.
4. The surgically debarked dog can still make noise, although the noise is not as loud as, nor does it sound like, a normal bark. Many people find the "bark" of a debarked dog disturbing because it sounds very hoarse and painful.
5. The debarked dog can't bark normally when you want it to. Your debarked dog will never warn off an intruder. The trespasser won't recognize the noise as a watchdog.

To sum up the situation, there are better ways to silence the barking dog than to cut its vocal chords.

The Use of Adverse Conditioning

To teach a dog not to bark, something unpleasant must happen to the dog *at the exact time* it barks, and *every* time it barks when it shouldn't. This is true with both the dog that barks from watchdog instinct and the dog that barks from confinement frustration. The use of *adverse conditioning* (punishment) for the puppy that cries when it is alone is cruel, is completely inappropriate, and should never be done. After all, it's only a baby.

To stop the nuisance barking of an older dog, adverse conditioning must take place when nobody is around. The negative stimulus must be unpleasant enough to the dog that it won't repeat the barking behavior. The stimulus must occur at the exact same time as the dog barks and every time the dog barks. There are several training devices on the market that do all this, and while they aren't exactly inexpensive, the devices cost much less than debarking surgery, or even less than a new dog.

The Bark Collar

The best of these anti-barking devices is the electronic battery-operated "bark" collar. There are several forms of these, and they are available in a wide range of prices. Electronic bark collars are actuated by the sound of the dog's bark, and they do one of three things: Some give the dog a low-voltage electric shock when it barks; some make an extremely shrill high-pitched noise that hurts the dog's ears when it barks; one model squirts the dog with a harmless chemical when it barks. Since they are electronically activated, the shock, the noise, or the chemical spray occurs *at the exact same time* as the bark. With only a very few barks, the dog learns to associate its barking with the unpleasant result. It's a rare dog that doesn't completely stop nuisance barking within ten minutes of wearing an effective electronic collar.

The best use of the electronic bark collar is as a preventive measure. If you find that your dog has the tendency to be a nuisance barker, get a collar and use it before the dog has made barking a habit, and before people start complaining about the noise. You can eliminate the problem before it ever develops.

Is this cruelty, to shock your dog or hurt its ears with a shrill noise when it barks? Consider this: Would you rather give up your dog than shock it a few times? Or would you rather keep your dog and have peace and quiet, both from your dog and from your neighbors. If you were a dog, would you rather receive a few unpleasant stimuli than lose your home, perhaps go to a shelter, and perhaps be killed there? You will be surprised at how few adverse stimuli it will take before your dog learns not to bark when it's wearing the collar—usually less than a half-dozen. And you can take the collar off when the dog is permitted to bark. The electronic anti-bark collar has saved the homes and the lives of many, many dogs.

The Crying Puppy

The little puppy that cries when first left alone in its Safe Space has a legitimate reason. It's frightened and lonely and it wants to find its mother. Nevertheless, every time you go to comfort it, you are providing positive reinforcement for its behavior; the only thing it wanted was company, and it got it by crying.

When a crying puppy hears you, it stops crying. You can't punish it for crying when it isn't crying because it will never understand. If you try to sit very quietly nearby so that you can yell the minute it makes a sound, you might be in for a very long night. The puppy will smell and hear you, will be reassured by your presence, and won't cry again until you sneak away.

You might think a shelter puppy would be used to being alone in a cage and not cry, but most of them will cry the first few nights. They might have been alone in their cage, but they heard and smelled many other dogs close by. If you get a puppy, you can put its little Safe Space next to your bed. After the puppy gets used to being in it and sleeps at night, you can then move it to the kitchen.

The best way to teach a puppy not to cry when left alone is to do nothing. Ignore it. Turn on your radio so you can't hear it. Then the crying puppy is not rewarded by your attention, and soon the crying behavior will stop from lack of positive reinforcement.

Chapter Eighteen
Essential Dog Equipment

Imagine a world in which no dog is ever hit by a car, and no dog is ever lost, stolen, or accidentally mated. In this imaginary world, no dog ever eats poison or is shot by an irate farmer down the road. What's the difference between the "real" world and this canine utopia? In the best of all dog worlds, dogs are never at large.

Dogs that Run Loose

Note: This is the most important statement in this book:

No dog should ever run loose.

Loose dogs fill the shelters with strays. Loose dogs produce unwanted litters. Millions of loose dogs are mangled by cars. Only owners who don't care about their dogs just open the door and simply let them run loose.

You wouldn't ever let your small children out on the streets alone with no provisions to keep them safe, and you wouldn't park your new Cadillac downtown with the keys in the ignition and the doors unlocked. Your children might get lost, hurt, or kidnapped, and you know your Cadillac wouldn't be there when you returned. Dogs are valuable too, but some owners have no hesitation to just open the door and let the dog out: "It'll come home when it's ready." Well, maybe it will, and maybe it won't. Maybe it's body will be spread all over the road by a car; maybe its throat will be torn out by a bigger dog; maybe it'll be taken home by someone who wants a dog just like that.

Most communities have laws prohibiting dogs from running loose. These laws were not made to protect dogs but to protect the community from the possible damage that dogs can cause. If the warden picks up your dog, you'll receive a significant fine, whether or not you get your dog back in one piece. If your dog digs up your fussy neighbors' shrubbery, you'll have a big bill from a landscaper; if it bites the neighbors child, you'll have a lawsuit.

If you had unlimited space and unlimited money, what kind of facilities would you provide for your dog? You'd have a big fenced yard, wouldn't you? You'd have a spacious Safe Space in the house or garage. You'd have a doggie door between the yard and the Safe Space so the dog could go in and out whenever it wanted. You might have another doggie door, a lockable one, between the dog's Safe Space and the rest of the house. You would be able to give your dog complete freedom or safe confinement indoors or out.

Unfortunately, most of us don't have the room or the money to have all these luxuries, but this doesn't mean we shouldn't have dogs. We must adjust our lives and our dogs' lives to fit our environment. We really need only a few things for successful dog ownership.

Do you have the space and money to fence a portion of your yard? Will you put your dog outside on a chain? Will you walk it on a leash? Decide these things before you select your dog, because the size and disposition of the dog will have a bearing on the success of your exercise facilities.

Fenced Yards

A fenced area in the yard is the best way to keep your dog at home. If the area is accessible from the back door, it's ideal. Once your dog is trained, all you have to do to let it out and in is to open the door.

If you decide on a fence, you must consider several things.

- Is the area near the road, and if it is, will passing traffic encourage the dog to bark?
- Can you erect a solid portion, like a stockade fence, so the dog can't see the neighbors?
- If you live in a city, check your zoning before you build anything; some places require permits for fences as well as for buildings.

Most fences designed to confine dogs are four feet high (1.2 m), and most dogs will be safely confined by them. However, large dogs that are determined to escape will get over a four-foot fence. Very few dogs can jump that high, but all dogs can climb a low wire fence, as well as a

A group of dogs can be safely confined together.

145

Digging under the fence is a problem with fences built around grass yards. Dog books tell you to bury a foot (.3 m) of wire, or to bend a portion of the fence at right angles so that it lies on the ground on the inside of the enclosure, and then to bury that horizontal portion of the wire. This requires extra labor and expense, but since most dogs will dig or crawl under fences if they get a chance, a solution must be found. A common solution is to place large rocks or cement blocks along the base of the fence. They must be heavy enough that your dog can't scratch them aside.

solid fence if they can get their front feet on the top of it. It depends on your dog's disposition—hunting breeds such as retrievers and pointers scale four-foot fences with ease, while shepherds and collies often stay behind them.

To confine a determined escapee, you can do several things. First, of course, is to build a higher fence. You aren't likely to want to do this for reasons of cost and appearance. A six-foot (1.8 m) fence would be very expensive and would make your yard look like a prison camp. You can keep a talented fence climber inside a four-foot (1.2 m) fence if you run an electric wire connected to a low-voltage shock unit a foot (.3 m) from the top on the inside of the fence. You only need to leave this unit on for a day or so; after a few shocks, your dog will never go near the fence.

Dog Runs

The dog run or pen built on a firm, easily cleaned surface is an option to a fenced yard. Although this gives your dog a limited area outside, it can be hidden somewhere inconspicuous on your property, such as behind the garage.

Surface Material for Dog Runs

Concrete: A poured concrete slab is the best surface for your run, since concrete is easy to clean up and hose off. If you choose a concrete pad, you can either have the run embedded in the concrete at the time it is poured, or buy a prefabricated chain-link dog run and set it up when the pad is dry. You can even set a dog run on an existing patio, if it is in a convenient location.

If you have a pad poured, be sure to insist on sufficient slope to provide good drainage when you wash it with the hose. One inch "fall" for every foot of concrete is minimum. No, your dog won't look like its living on the side of a hill. In fact you won't even notice the slope until you see the water run off.

Concrete pads poured for dog runs should not be finished perfectly smooth, especially in cold climates, as they become slippery ice rinks in the winter, which is hard on the dogs as well as on the people who have to clean them. The best surface is what the industry calls a "very light brush finish." This is rough enough to not be slippery but smooth enough to be easily cleaned.

Patio Blocks: A perfectly satisfactory surface for a dog run is one made of patio blocks, placed so the spaces between them are as narrow as possible. Discarded concrete sidewalk slabs also have been used with great success, as have second-hand bricks, placed close together. This kind of run surface will need to be installed on a gravel or sand foundation, to prevent sinking and shifting of the material.

Gravel: A gravel surface for a dog run is far less expensive and far easier to install than are surfaces of concrete or block, but it is much less satisfactory. Every time stools are picked up, some gravel is also removed, necessitating frequent replenishing of the gravel supply. Furthermore, gravel runs can't be hosed adequately, and

some dogs will eat gravel out of boredom.

Grass: Grass surfaced runs are the least satisfactory, because they will soon become bare ground, and then turn to mud the first time it rains. If you are going to build a dog run, try to devise a better surface for it than grass.

Prefabricated Panel Runs: Prefabricated panel runs are easily taken down and moved, and are sturdy enough to contain any dog, but they have one disadvantage over runs that are set in concrete. A big dog jumping on the fence can shift the entire run a few inches, and if the concrete is poured to the exact dimensions of the run, a big dog will knock the corner of the run off the pad. If your run is not to be set into the concrete, have your pad poured a little bigger than the dimensions of your run.

A home-made dog run is very satisfactory.

Commercial Runs: Commercial dog runs are supplied in varying lengths but are usually four-feet wide and six-feet high (1.2 by 1.8 m) Even if you set up a six-foot high pen, some dogs will climb it. To climb a fence, a dog has to have a running start. Dogs can't climb the long sides of a standard run because the standard width is too narrow for them to get a good start. This means that you can keep your climber in its run by making an overhang on the insides of only the short ends. You don't need to install overhangs on the long sides.

Alternatives to Fences

Most dog owners don't have a fenced yard. Fences are expensive; fences are permanent; fences are not even allowed in some communities. But don't think you shouldn't have a dog unless you can have a fence.

Many house dogs are taken outside entirely on a leash. This is fine if you have the time to do it and you're willing to go out in all sorts of weather, night and day. If your dog is trained to obey off-leash, you can even take it to a park where it can run around.

Chains

Once your dog is housebroken, you can install a chain that reaches to its bathroom area and snap the chain on the dog's collar when it needs to go out to eliminate. If the bathroom area is near your house, you can attach one end of the chain very near the door and just step outside to attach the dog. You can walk your dog on a leash only for exercise. This is a good idea in communities that have pooper-scooper laws that require owners to clean up after their dogs. Chaining your dog outside to eliminate is appropriate *only* after the dog has learned about the outside bathroom area and is used to the confinement of a chain. Until your new dog is housebroken, take it out on a leash and stand there to make sure it does what it's supposed to do.

Chains made for dogs are usually of wire twisted into figure-eight links. These have a snap on each end and a swivel in the center to prevent kinking, and can be purchased in a variety of lengths and weights suitable for any size dog. The links are just about the same in cheap and expensive chains of the same length and weight, but the swivel and snaps on inexpensive chains are often made out of light, weak metal. If your dog breaks a chain, it's usually at a flimsy tongue snap or a cheap swivel. If you get an inexpensive chain, keep your eye on the hardware; you might need to replace it. All chains will rust, of course, so inspect yours after a few months outside.

Dog Trolleys

To give your dog a little more room to move around, you can

stretch a wire cable between two stationary objects such as two trees, two buildings, or a building and a tree. Then you can snap the dog's chain onto a pulley that slides along the wire. You can buy ready-made dog equipment of this type, called dog trolleys, at pet stores, pet departments in discount stores, or from catalogs, or you can make your own. The equipment is usually inexpensive to buy ready made, so it isn't cost effective to make your own if you have to buy the cable and turn-buckles needed to keep it tight. The trolley arrangement gives your chained dog more room and allows you to keep the bathroom area farther from the house. You'll find that if either end of the wire is attached to a tree or post, the dog will get its chain wrapped around it, so you might have to place an obstruction on the wire so the dog can't pull its chain close enough to run around the trees. Commercial trolleys sometimes come with clamps for this purpose.

Tree Trolleys

A dog chained only to a tree is soon hopelessly tangled around it. To prevent this, you can place a circle of cable or chain at least twice the diameter of the tree loosely around the base of the trunk and attach the dog's chain to this circle. That way, the dog pulls its chain around the tree on the circle instead of tangling it. The circle must be much larger than the trunk, and if it is to surround a living tree, it should

This tree-trolley was made with a long chain and an old vacuum cleaner hose. It will not tangle

be run through an old piece of garden hose or something similar to keep the wire from damaging the bark. This device is called a tree trolley by the commercial manufacturer that makes it. The commercial one does not have a hose on the circle to protect your shade tree, so if you buy one, add the hose before you use it.

Tie Out Stakes

Pet stores and hardware stores sell stakes with a swivel on top for owners to pound or turn into the ground for a tie out. Don't use one of these for a strong dog or in soft ground, or you might find your dog trotting down the street dragging its stake.

The Collar

If you're going to chain your dog outside, it's usually best to use a plain, flat collar that fits tight enough that the dog can't back out of it. Get a thick collar for a large dog.

Double-ply nylon is best; leather might stretch if it gets wet. Some short-coated, small-headed dogs such as dobermans and dachshunds will escape from surprisingly tight collars. Never use a choke chain or a nylon cord choke collar to tie a dog, as these can twist and strangle a dog. A heavy, *flat* nylon choke is a good choice for escape artists, but these collars must be adjusted to fit as snug as a buckle collar. Practically any determined dog can wiggle its way out of a harness.

The Leash

When you buy a leash, get a six-footer (1.8 m). If you want a longer one, you can buy one or you can use a piece of clothesline. Nylon or fabric leashes are less expensive and more durable than leather. Don't tie your dog with a leash or rope—any self-respecting dog can chew through them. And don't use a chain for a leash, as it will hurt your hands when the dog pulls.

Dog Doors

For owners who want their dogs to come in and go out at will, there are a great variety of dog doors on the market. You can select from catalogs such features as locking, one-way, even magnetic-coded so only your own dog, wearing a special collar, can go through them. A great many dogs will not realize that they can go through the flap of a dog door; you have to teach them by propping or tying the door up for a day or two, then going just outside the door and calling them with a treat. After they once take the plunge and go through the flap, most dogs will do it again without hesitation.

The Safe Space

As discussed in previous chapters, a Safe Space is an area inside the house in which a dog can be confined in safety and comfort. The most common form of a Safe Space is a wire cage. If your dog isn't too big, a wire cage is fine, but if you get a full-grown shepherd, you will have to buy an enormous cage or build your own pen.

A cage or pen intended for a dog's permanent Safe Space should be big enough for the adult dog to lie down in comfort, and it should be high enough that the dog's head doesn't hit the top. It should be strong enough that the dog can't tear it apart, and most dogs will test this. A Safe Space should admit daylight, as no dog likes to be confined in the dark. Plastic airline carriers can be used if arranged so light gets in through the door, but most of these are too small for a permanent Safe Space, and the huge ones cost more than a good wire cage.

If you have a full-time job, your dog's Safe Space needs to be bigger than if you are home to let it out frequently. If a dog is to spend eight hours or more at a time in it, its Safe Space should be large enough for it to be able to move around a little, chew on a few toys, and have a drink of water. In general, the

This cage with a broken front cost $3.00 at a local garage sale.

The broken front has been removed and a new front of the same size was drawn onto quarter-inch plywood. The door and frame will be cut out of the same piece.

The door was cut out of the center of the frame piece. The saber saw was started in a hole drilled under the location for a hinge.

The new front was assembled with two hinges and a latch. It was then stapled on to the body of the cage.

Safe Space for a dog that's going to spend a lot of time there should be twice as big as one intended only to be the dog's bed.

Wire Cages

Wire cages are available in pet stores, feed stores, and some discount stores, but they are not inexpensive. The quality of wire cages varies greatly, and you get what you pay for. The main problem with cheap cages is that they are not very strong. If you buy a toy breed, you can get a cheap cage, but if you buy a large breed, you'll find that your

For a short dog, the cage can be used horizontally, providing a larger floor space.

dog can bend the wires or break the door of a poorly constructed cage. Flimsy cages have large spaces between the wires and high-gauge wire. (The higher the gauge, the thinner the wire; eleven-gauge is thinner than nine-gauge.) Most dog cages are made with relatively heavy horizontal wires interspersed with finer vertical wires, and with narrower horizontal than vertical spacing. It's the long, weak vertical wires that dogs can get their teeth around. A big, determined dog can make scrap out of cages with thin wire and four-inch (10 cm) spacing. A good, big dog cage should be made with seven- or nine-gauge wires horizontally and at least eleven-gauge wires vertically, and with as narrow spacing between the wires as you can afford.

The very best dog cages are constructed of heavy wire mesh with one-inch (2.5 cm.) spacing both horizontally and vertically. These are the strongest you can buy because dogs can't get their jaws into the small spaces to chew the wires. These cages are available from mail

order catalogs in a large variety of sizes and shapes. Although they cost a little more, they'll far outlast the flimsier cages; in fact, they might outlast several dogs.

A surprising number of cages are sold at local garage sales, often at very low prices, and if you don't like the price, you can always make an offer. Many garage sale cages show signs of hard use—usually the bottom tray is damaged or missing and the door is in poor repair. Trays can be replaced with a piece of plywood or tempered masonite, even many layers of newspapers. If you are the least bit handy, you can make a new front for a cage from a piece of quarter-inch plywood the same size as the damaged front. If you are careful when you cut out the square doorway, you can hinge the piece you removed back on to make the door.

Making Your Own Cage or Pen

If you get a very large dog and you intend to leave it in its Space for a long time, you might not be able to get a big enough cage. You need to make some sort of a pen it can't get out of. If you want to spend a few dollars, you can buy a small free standing chain-link dog run and set it up in any area indoors that is dry and light. These runs come in the form of four panels, one with a door in it, and corner clamps to hold the panels together. Anyone can assemble these runs in a few minutes. A nice little run won't cost much more than a really good cage, and will be larger and more sturdy. Sometimes, dog runs and pens are for sale second hand; look in the Pets column of your local paper.

It takes a little more skill with a saw and hammer to build your own pen, but you don't have to be a carpenter to do it. You can even make your own pen or cage panels from plywood by making cut outs in the plywood and covering them with heavy hardware cloth or wire fence material. Buy wire with one-by-one or one-by-two-inch spacing. Always put the wire on the inside, to prevent your dog from chewing the wooden edges. You can join these panels with loose-pin hinges so you can pull the pins and fold up the pen if you need to. Use your ingenuity.

Depending on your living arrangements, you often can devise a simple pen by closing off the end of a hallway with a commercial or homemade dog gate. You might even get by with using a completely empty small utility room for your dog's Safe Space, especially if you buy an older dog that is really almost ready to be trusted alone in the house. Keep this in mind: Dogs can and will chew toilet seats.

If you choose a very young puppy, you can, of course, keep it temporarily in a cardboard box. Very soon, however, it will outgrow anything except a refrigerator carton, and cardboard is flimsy and not washable. When you build or buy a permanent Safe Space, make it big enough for the dog to use when it is an adult; you don't want to go to all that trouble and expense more than once.

How high must the sides of a pen be? If a dog or puppy can jump up and get its feet to the top, it can climb over. Some dogs are more motivated to escape than others; you'll soon find out if your dog is adept at climbing out. Cages, of course, have a top. You might have to make a top for your pen if your dog is an escape artist.

Dogs like to play with children's toys.

Important Hints on Dog Care

Here are a few more things you might want to know:

Cleaning Up

Many city owners don't know how to dispose of the dog stools they clean up in their yard. If your dog isn't too gigantic, if you clean up fairly regularly, and if you don't mind carrying the mess into the house, flushing them down the toilet is a good solution. You can always wrap them *very* well and put them in the trash, but if the pickup discovers the mess in your trash, they might refuse to collect at your house. Commercial stool disposers designed to be sunk into the ground are available from catalogs. They use enzymes to digest the waste and allow it to leach out into the soil. Unless you have very sandy soil, you'll have to dig a huge hole and partly fill it with gravel to get a good leach bed, and you'll always have to have a supply of enzymes. Except in the best of conditions, these stool disposers don't work well enough to make them worth the trouble.

Commercial Dog Repellents

Commercial dog repellents in paint-on or spray cans are supposed to keep dogs from chewing things they shouldn't. Don't trust them to protect anything you value. Sometimes they work; sometimes they don't. Spray-on repellents for ornamental plants outdoors last only until it rains, then they have to be reapplied.

Keep Your Dog Safe in a Car

To control your dog in the car, harnesses are available that buckle onto seat belts and keep your dog as secure as a human passenger. If you want to continue to close your dog's leash in the door to keep it in one place, but you want the dog to be safe in case of a crash, you can attach the leash to a well-fitting harness instead of the dog's collar. Automobile and station wagon barriers can be purchased to fit all vehicles.

Head Collars and Muzzles

Fairly new on the market are head collars that look like a horse's halter, and other anti-pulling devices for big, strong dogs. If you need a muzzle for your dog, get a cone-shaped one of leather or fabric to fit your dog, not one made only of straps. Strap muzzles have to be extremely tight to be effective.

Whatever you think you need, someone makes it. It's a good idea to see some of these fancy apparatuses in use before you spend a lot of money on them. Basically, all you need for your dog is a collar, a leash, something to hold its food and water, and, of course, a nice Safe Space.

Chapter Nineteen
The Future—
Better or Worse?

There is a disease that kills ten million dogs a year. It affects puppies and older dogs alike, females and males, big breeds and small. At least ten percent of the dog population is at risk of catching this disease and dying from it.

If such a disease were caused by a new virus, dog owners would be in an uproar. Veterinary schools would request huge sums for research, epidemiologists would study the spread of the disease and devise plans to control it, and veterinarians' appointment books would be jammed with clients wanting to bring their dogs for "shots" to protect them.

There is such a disease, but it is not caused by a virus. It is the canine *Nobody-Wants-Me* disease, and it is very often fatal to the dogs that catch it.

Two groups of dogs are especially vulnerable to being affected with this condition. The first group consists of puppies of unplanned and unwanted litters. The second group is the adult or near-adult dogs that "didn't work out" and are relinquished to animal shelters.

More than two-thirds of these dogs die because nobody wants them.

Progress is being made to alleviate this situation in the United States. In spite of the increase n the pet population, the number of dogs killed annually at shelters is actually on the decrease. This happy fact is largely due to the efforts of national humane organizations and the American Veterinary Medical Association, which together have conducted a media campaign to promote the sterilization of pet dogs, not only for population control, but for the health of each individual animal. Humane societies distribute educational material. Veterinarians recommend surgical neutering to their clients as part of every well-dog routine. Increasing numbers of animal welfare groups and shelters subsidize the cost of sterilization or offer for adoption only those dogs that have been sterilized. Early-age spay and neuter programs prevent pups with reproductive potential from entering the community. Municipal spay-neuter clinics have made low-cost surgery available to more pet owners.

A wonderful old companion.

Is this enough? Many people in the animal control industry don't think so. Attempts to legislate against random reproduction in the pet population have met with little success. Antibreeding laws and differential cost of licensing of altered and unaltered dogs have been perceived as attacks on breeders of purebreds and unnecessary infringement on individuals' rights.

Humane organizations argue that if fewer dogs were born, there would be a greater chance that each of them could get a home. This is obviously a true statement, but it addresses only part of the problem.

Why do so many adult and young adult dogs end up at shelters? Changes in the lives of their owners necessitate the relinquishment of some of the dogs, but in the majority of cases, the dogs' owners have not succeeded in teaching their puppies how to grow into socially acceptable dogs.

Humane organizations, veterinarians, animal control officers, teachers, breed clubs, and all members of the media are joining to educate the dog-owning public, not only how to prevent the birth of pups for which there are no homes, but how to raise each puppy to be an asset rather than a possibly dangerous and destructive liability.

Everyone who buys a shelter dog and gives it a loving home makes a difference. Every shelter dog that is allowed to rejoin society as a valued companion represents one more life *saved.*

Useful Information

Organizations

American Humane
Association (AHA)
63 Inverness Drive East
Englewood, Colorado 80112
(303) 792-9900

The American Kennel Club (AKC)
5580 Centerview Drive, Suite 200
Raleigh, North Carolina
27606-3390
(919) 233-9767

American Society for the
Prevention of Cruelty to Animals
(ASPCA)
National Headquarters
424 East 92nd Street
New York, New York 10128
(212) 876-7700

Delta Society
PO Box 1080
Renton, Washington 98057-9906
(206) 226-7357

Humane Society of the United
States (HSUS)
2100 L Street, NW
Washington, D.C. 20037
(202) 452-1100

National Animal Control Association
PO Box 480851
Kansas City, Missouri 64148-0851

Further Reading

Books

Bailey, Gwen, *The Perfect Puppy.*
Reader's Digest Association, Inc.
Pleasantville, New York, 1995.
Journal of the American Veterinary
Medical Association, *Zoonosis
Updates, 2nd Edition.* AVMA,
Schaumburg, Illinois.

This dachshund-mix will become a wonderful house dog.

Klever, Ulrich. *The Complete Book of Dog Care.* Barron's Educational Series, Inc., Hauppauge, New York, 1989.

Ross, John and Barbara McKinney. *Puppy Preschool: Raising Your Puppy Right-From the Start.* St. Martin's Press, New York, New York, 1996.

Siegal, Mordecai, ed. *University of California Davis Book of Dogs: A Complete Medical Reference Guide for Dogs and Puppies.* HarperCollins Inc., New York, New York, 1995.

Weber, Shirley. *Project BREED: A National Sourcebook for Rescue and Adoption of all Breeds of Dogs.* Germantown, Maryland, 1993.

Wrede, Barbara. *Civilizing Your Puppy.* Barron's Educational Series, Hauppauge, New York, 1992.

Periodicals

Advocate, A Magazine of the AMH Animal Protection Division
(Quarterly to AHA Members)
American Humane Association
63 Inverness Drive East
Englewood, Colorado 80112

ASPCA Animal Watch
(Quarterly to ASPCA members)
American Society for the Prevention of Cruelty to Animals
424 East 92nd Street
New York, NY 10128-6804

HSUS News
(Quarterly to HSUS members)
Humane Society of the United States
2100 L Street, NW
Washington, DC 20037

Shelter Sense
(10 issues a year to HSUS members)
Humane Society of the United States
2100 L Street, NW
Washington, DC 20037

Shoptalk for Animal Care and Control Professionals
(Quarterly to AHA professional members)
American Humane Association
63 Inverness Drive East
Englewood, Colorado 80112

Index

M091370577